P9-CSB-773

TREASURY OF Bible Stories

Contributing Writers
Marlene Targ Brill
Gary Burge
Etta G. Wilson

Consultant
David M. Howard, Jr., Ph.D.

Cover Illustration
Karen Pritchett

Book Illustrations
Thomas Gianni
Lyn Martin
Karen Pritchett
Cheryl Roberts
Sally Schaedler
Gary Torrisi

PUBLICATIONS INTERNATIONAL, LTD.

David M. Howard, Jr., Ph.D. (consultant) is an associate professor of Old Testament and Semitic Languages and is a member of the Society of Biblical Literature and the Institute for Biblical Research.

Louis Weber, C.E.O.
Publications International, Ltd.
7373 North Cicero Avenue
Lincolnwood, Illinois 60646

Manufactured in the U.S.A.

8 7 6 5 4 3 2 1

ISBN: 0–7853–1113–0

Library of Congress Catalog Card Number: 94–69614

CONTENTS

The Creation

In the beginning, there was nothing but God alone. So God decided to create the world.

On the first day, God spoke and he made the vast universe and its many planets. Among the planets was Earth. But everything was dark and cold. Even Earth had no plants, no animals, no life. God spoke again and said, "Let there be light," and the universe was filled with light shining from every corner.

On the second day, God looked at Earth and decided to create even more. God spoke again, and this time he made the air and the sky that surrounds Earth like a blue-gray blanket. There was water everywhere on the planet, so he took some of it to make the clouds. God looked at his work and said, "This is good."

On the third day, God separated the water from the land. Mountains rose from the seas. Rolling hills formed in the vast plains. Volcanoes exploded and deep valleys opened as the land moved. Gentle rains fell on the land and soon rivers were rushing down the hills, finding a path to the seas.

God said that the ground should grow plants! Forests and jungles sprang to life. Grasses and fruit trees, bushes and flowers began to cover the land. God liked it all and he said it was good.

On the fourth day, God marked off day and night with the sun and moon. The daytime would be embraced by the sun's warm rays. The night sky would be lit by the moon and stars God had sprinkled in the sky. God enjoyed the beauty of the wonders he had created. Again he said it was good.

On the fifth day God decided to fill up the places he had made on the second day. In the sky, he put uncountable numbers of birds. Hummingbirds and robins, eagles and hawks swooped through the air.

God also made creatures to live in the water. He spoke again and soon the seas were teeming with fish, whales, eels, crabs, and sharks. God blessed them all and told them to have many children to fill the oceans and rivers of the world.

On the sixth day God decided to fill the land he had made on the third day. He said, "Let the land bring me animals of every kind!" Soon reptiles and spiders crawled everywhere. Animals that walked on four legs and animals that swung through the trees, gigantic creatures and tiny ones, filled the land. God liked what he was making. He said once more, "This is good."

When Earth brought forth animals, God decided to do something special, something only he could do. God took the soil of the ground and shaped it gently. He made a new and beautiful creature. Then he breathed into it and made a human for the first time.

God wanted humans to be like him. He worked some more and made both man and woman. They were partly like Earth and partly like God. The first man was called Adam and the first woman was named Eve. God blessed them and told them to have many children.

God told Adam and Eve to take care of the world. "You are responsible for every living thing. The trees and the seeds of the grass will give you food, but you must protect them." Adam and Eve promised to obey.

On the seventh day, God decided to rest. The world was beautiful to look at, and he delighted in his creation. The snow-capped mountains were filled with wildlife. Blue oceans teemed with fish. Shimmering deserts and steaming jungles showed the wonder and variety of God's imagination. The air was fresh and clear, and the flapping of wings and singing of birds filled the sky. The world was at peace. No one hurt anyone else.

God made this seventh day different from all the rest. He blessed it just like he blessed the rest of his creation. Forever this would be God's day, a day to rest and think about him and his good work. Today, this is why every week we stop what we do and spend one day resting and worshiping God.

God planted a beautiful garden for Adam and Eve to live in. He called it the Garden of Eden. In the garden was every kind of plant.

Adam and Eve were happy in the garden. They were good friends with the animals. They were never hungry or cold or sick. Like the animals, they did not wear clothes and were not ashamed. Adam and Eve never worried about anything. They loved the Lord deeply and they loved each other.

In the garden God let them do anything they wanted. But he made one rule. In the middle of the garden was a tree unlike any of the others. It was the Tree of the Knowledge of Good and Evil. Adam and Eve were not allowed to eat fruit from this tree. As long as they obeyed, God would know how much they trusted and loved him.

One afternoon Adam and Eve were walking in the middle of the Garden of Eden. The devil disguised as a snake spoke to Eve. "Did God really say you can't eat any fruit from any tree?" he asked.

"No," replied Eve, "just this tree. God said if I do I will die! That tree is not for us!"

But the snake argued back, "God was lying. If you eat it you will become like God. You will know what is good and what is evil."

Eve had never disobeyed God before. But the snake kept talking. And Eve kept thinking and wanting—and soon she grabbed a piece of fruit from a branch. She took a mouthful. Then she gave the fruit to Adam and he took a bite, too.

At once, Adam and Eve felt different. They looked at their bodies and felt ashamed to be naked. They found some fig leaves and sewed them together to cover themselves.

Suddenly, Adam and Eve heard the Lord coming. They hid behind some bushes. God called out, "Where are you?" He knew something was wrong.

Adam said, "Eve made me do it." Eve said the snake had made her do it. Each tried to get out of trouble. But Adam and Eve had both sinned.

God saw the snake slipping through the grass. He thundered angrily, "Because you have done this, you are the lowest among all the animals. Friendship between you and humans will disappear. And someday, a human will come along to destroy you forever."

Then the Lord spoke to Adam and Eve one at a time. To Eve he said, "This terrible decision has ruined our life together. You did not believe me but chose to follow your own thoughts instead. Now life will become hard for you. Even your life with Adam will not be easy anymore."

To Adam the Lord said, "You too have sinned. And because you decided not to follow me with your whole heart, life outside Eden will be hard for you too. From now on, you will have to work hard to get food."

But God still loved Adam and Eve. God killed the first animal and made them clothes to cover them better. Then he sent them out of the garden. He sent an angel to stand at the garden entrance with a flaming sword so that they could not go back in.

Adam and Eve were very sad and they cried for all that they had lost. But they went out from the garden and found a patch of land to settle on. There they built their house and farmed the land.

Life was much harder than in Eden, but Adam and Eve still had each other. Soon, they had children, too. And, even though he had thrown them out of the Garden of Eden, God continued to love Adam and Eve and all their children. But things have never been the same as they were in the beginning.

Noah's Ark

One day, many years after God created Adam and Eve, he looked closely at all the people on earth. There were many more people now. They had forgotten about God and his ways.

"I see only evil in people's hearts," God said sadly. "I am sorry that I made them." God grew more and more unhappy about this. He then decided to start all over again.

God had one faithful servant named Noah. Noah and his family loved God. God wanted to save Noah and his family. So, God said to Noah, "I am going to put an end to all things as they are now."

Meanwhile, God told Noah to bring two of each living thing to the ark. This was a very big job. Noah and his family were going to have to take care of all the animals while they were on the ark. There were big and small animals, strong and weak animals, insects and birds of all kinds. Every type of animal you can think of was going to go on the ark!

Once all the animals were together, God told Noah to take clothing and food for their journey. Some food was for Noah and his family to eat. Some was for the animals. And some was to store for after the flood.

Noah did all that God ordered.

Later, God spoke to Noah again. He said, "Go into the ark now, you and all who are with you. In seven days I will send rain on the earth. The rain will last forty days and forty nights. Water will wash away everything from the ground."

Noah followed God's instructions. He loaded all of the animals into the ark and put all the food and clothes inside the ark. Finally, Noah and his family entered the ark. This was the last time they would be on dry land for a very long time.

On the seventh day, God shut the ark. Rain began to fall to earth.

At first drops of rain fell here and there. But it was not long before great waves of water pounded the ground. Soon, large puddles formed. Streams turned into rivers. Rivers turned into oceans.

The water began to get higher and higher. Floodwater was so strong it lifted the ark above the earth. People and animals ran for high places. But there seemed to be water everywhere! Soon water covered every tree and mountain top.

Only Noah and those who were with him in the ark had a safe place to stay.

The ark floated along safely. Inside, Noah and his family were safe and warm. They took care of the animals. The rain came down for forty days and forty nights. All that could be seen for miles and miles was water and cloudy skies.

But God had not forgotten about Noah and the good people and creatures on the ark. God caused a strong wind to blow the clouds apart. The rain stopped. A bright sun came out and started to dry up all the floodwaters.

Little by little, the water went down. Before too long, the tops of mountains could be seen peeking through the water. God caused the ark to rest on top of a mountain called Ararat.

One day, Noah opened the ark window and sent out a raven. The raven saw nothing but water. There was no place for the bird to land. One week later, Noah sent out a dove. The dove had to return to the ark because there still wasn't a place to land. Noah waited another week and sent the dove out again. This time, the dove came back with a leaf from an olive tree. Noah knew that enough water was gone for trees to grow again.

After one more week, Noah sent the dove out again. This time it did not return. The bird had found a place to build a nest. Now Noah knew that all the floodwater had dried up.

Noah removed the door from the ark. Imagine what he saw! There, after such a long time with nothing but water everywhere, Noah could see land! There were mountains and plains, hills and valleys. Even the rivers and lakes were normal again.

Then Noah heard God speak to him. "You have done as I commanded," God said. "Now leave the ark with your family. Bring out all the living things you cared for during the flood. Let them live on earth and grow in numbers."

So Noah and everyone on the ark did as God ordered.

They were all happy to step onto dry land again. They felt thankful that God had taken such good care of them. They wanted to thank God for all these things. So, they built an altar and prayed. They offered their thanks to God for their safety.

God heard Noah's prayers. Right then, God made a promise in his heart:

"I will never destroy the ground because of evil in the human heart. I will never destroy almost every living creature as I have done. From now on, you will plant seeds and harvest crops. There will be summer and winter and day and night. I will give you everything you need for your family to grow large and strong."

God repeated this promise to Noah. "Never again shall I flood the earth." Then God sent a beautiful rainbow across the sky.

"This first rainbow is a sign of my word. Other rainbows will remind you and all future people of my promise. Whenever a rainbow appears in the clouds, I will see it and remember my promise."

Joseph's Coat of Many Colors

Long ago, in the land of Canaan, lived a man named Jacob. He had many animals. He also had many children. Of all his children, Jacob loved Joseph best. To show his love, Jacob made a bright and colorful robe. Then he gave it to his favorite son.

Joseph had ten older brothers. When they found out that their father had given Joseph this special gift, they became jealous. Later, Joseph had two dreams. When he told his brothers about the dreams, they became even more upset. Joseph said the dreams showed that his brothers would some day bow down to him. "You think your dreams mean you will rule over us," his brothers said angrily.

Soon after Joseph's dreams, the brothers had to go to take care of the animals in the fields. They were gone for a long time. Jacob told Joseph, "Go and see if your brothers and the flock are well. Then come back and tell me what you heard."

When the brothers saw Joseph walking toward them, they saw he was wearing his special robe. They got angry all over again.

When Joseph reached them, they ripped off his robe. They threw him into an empty pit and sat down to eat. A group of traders passed by their flock. One brother said, "Let's sell our brother to these traders. We will get money and he will live."

The brothers pulled Joseph out of the pit. They sold their brother to the traders for money. But what would they tell their father? They killed a goat and dipped the coat into the blood. Then they took the coat to their father.

"It is my son's coat," Jacob cried. "A wild animal must have killed him." Jacob wept and wept. He was so sad, nothing could make him feel better.

Meanwhile, Joseph had been sold as a slave in Egypt But God was watching over him. A court official named Potiphar bought Joseph and put him in charge of all he owned. Then one day Joseph was blamed for something he didn't do. But Potiphar did not believe Joseph.

In fact, Potiphar was so angry, he had Joseph thrown into the Pharaoh's prison. Joseph shared a cell with two men who had been the Pharaoh's baker and chief cupbearer.

During that time, the cupbearer had a dream. Joseph explained it to him. What Joseph said came true. Soon, Pharaoh forgave the cupbearer and returned him to his palace job.

Joseph spent two more years in jail. But God took care of him there. One night, Pharaoh had two dreams that troubled him. But there was no one in Egypt who could explain the dreams. Finally, the cupbearer remembered Joseph. He told Pharaoh about the young man who was able to explain what dreams mean.

Pharaoh sent for Joseph and had him listen to the dreams. "Both dreams mean the same thing, Pharaoh," Joseph said. "God told you what will happen. There will be seven good years. Crops will grow and food will be plentiful. Then there will be seven bad years. The land will be dry and no food will grow. Everyone will be very hungry."

Joseph suggested that Pharaoh select a wise man to collect food during the good years. The stored food would feed the people of Egypt during the bad years. Pharaoh liked the plan, so he put Joseph in charge. He ordered people to bow down to Joseph. Now only Pharaoh was greater among the people than Joseph.

Everything happened just as Joseph had said it would. During the next seven years, there was a wealth of crops. Joseph had the food gathered and stored. Then the seven years of plenty ended. During the next seven years, no food grew. People cried from hunger in every country. But there was bread throughout Egypt.

"Go to Joseph," Pharaoh told his people. "Do what he says." Joseph opened the filled and overflowing storehouses. He sold bread to people from all over the world.

Back in Canaan, Jacob and his family needed food, too. He sent his sons to Egypt to buy bread. But Jacob kept his youngest son, Benjamin, at home. He was afraid something bad might happen to him.

The brothers came to Joseph and bowed down. They did not recognize him, but Joseph recognized them! He pretended not to know them and asked who they were. "We are honest men from Canaan. We are twelve sons of one man. The youngest is with our father. One brother is no more."

Joseph had a plan. He said they were spies and sent them to prison for three days. When they were allowed to go home, Joseph said they had to leave one brother, Simeon, in Egypt. They were to bring Benjamin back to prove they were telling the truth.

Joseph had the money they used to buy grain put inside the bags. On the way home, they found the money. They were sure they would get in trouble!

When they got home, they told Jacob what happened. Jacob did not want to let Benjamin go back with them. But when the grain was gone, Jacob realized he had to let Benjamin go.

The brothers returned to Joseph. When he saw Benjamin, Joseph had to leave the room. He was happy and sad at the same time. They ate dinner and Joseph had the sacks of grain prepared. The servants put the money in them like before. But this time he had them hide a silver cup in Benjamin's sack.

The brothers started on their way home. Joseph sent guards to catch up with them. They told them that someone had stolen a silver cup. The brothers said, "We would never do that."

The guards searched the sacks. There was the silver cup! They took the brothers back to Joseph. The brothers fell to the ground before Joseph and begged him to let them go. Joseph agreed to let everyone go—everyone except Benjamin. Since the cup was in his sack, he was to stay as Joseph's servant.

"The boy's father will die without him," cried the brothers. Joseph couldn't keep the secret any longer. He told them who he was.

"Do not worry," Joseph told his troubled brothers. "It was God, not you, who sent me here. God made me Pharaoh's ruler over all the land to keep you alive." Joseph hugged Benjamin and wept. He kissed all his brothers.

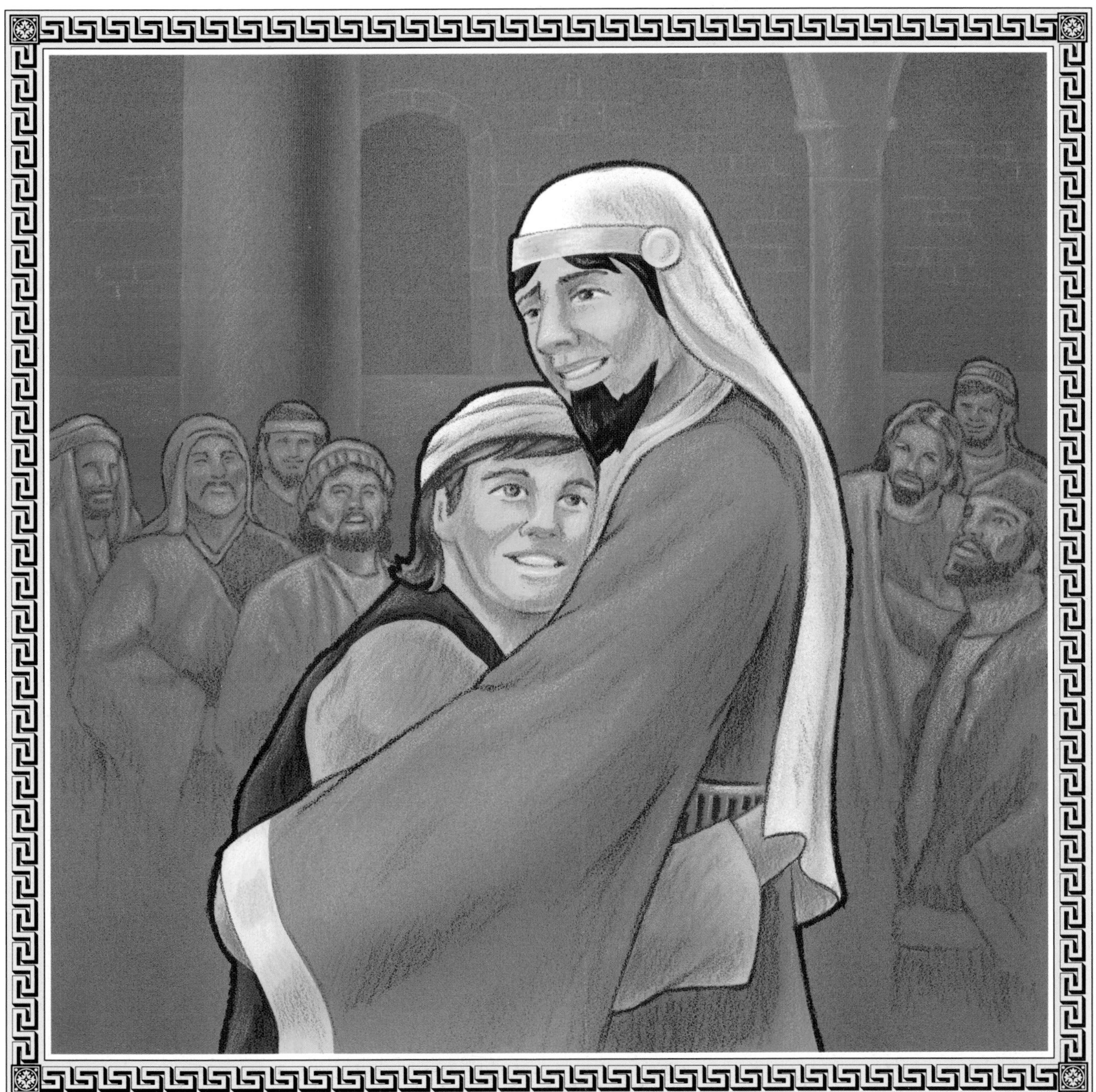

Pharaoh told Joseph to move the whole family to Egypt. Pharaoh said, "I will give you the best land."

Everyone in Jacob's family came to Egypt. Joseph greeted them. Jacob and Joseph were very happy to see each other again.

The Story of Moses:

Moses in Egypt

A long time ago, there was a terrible famine in the land of Israel. The crops would not grow and the people were starving. The people of Israel, the Israelites, decided to move to Egypt. There they lived in peace for more than 400 years.

Now in Egypt, kings were called Pharaohs. One day, a new Pharaoh became the ruler of Egypt. This Pharaoh hated the Israelites. He made them slaves and forced them to build palaces and cities for him. Men, women, and even children worked from morning till night in the heat of the sun. "Set us free," they cried out to the soldiers who guarded them. But no one listened.

Pharaoh was full of hatred for the Israelites. He ordered that all newborn Israelite children should die.

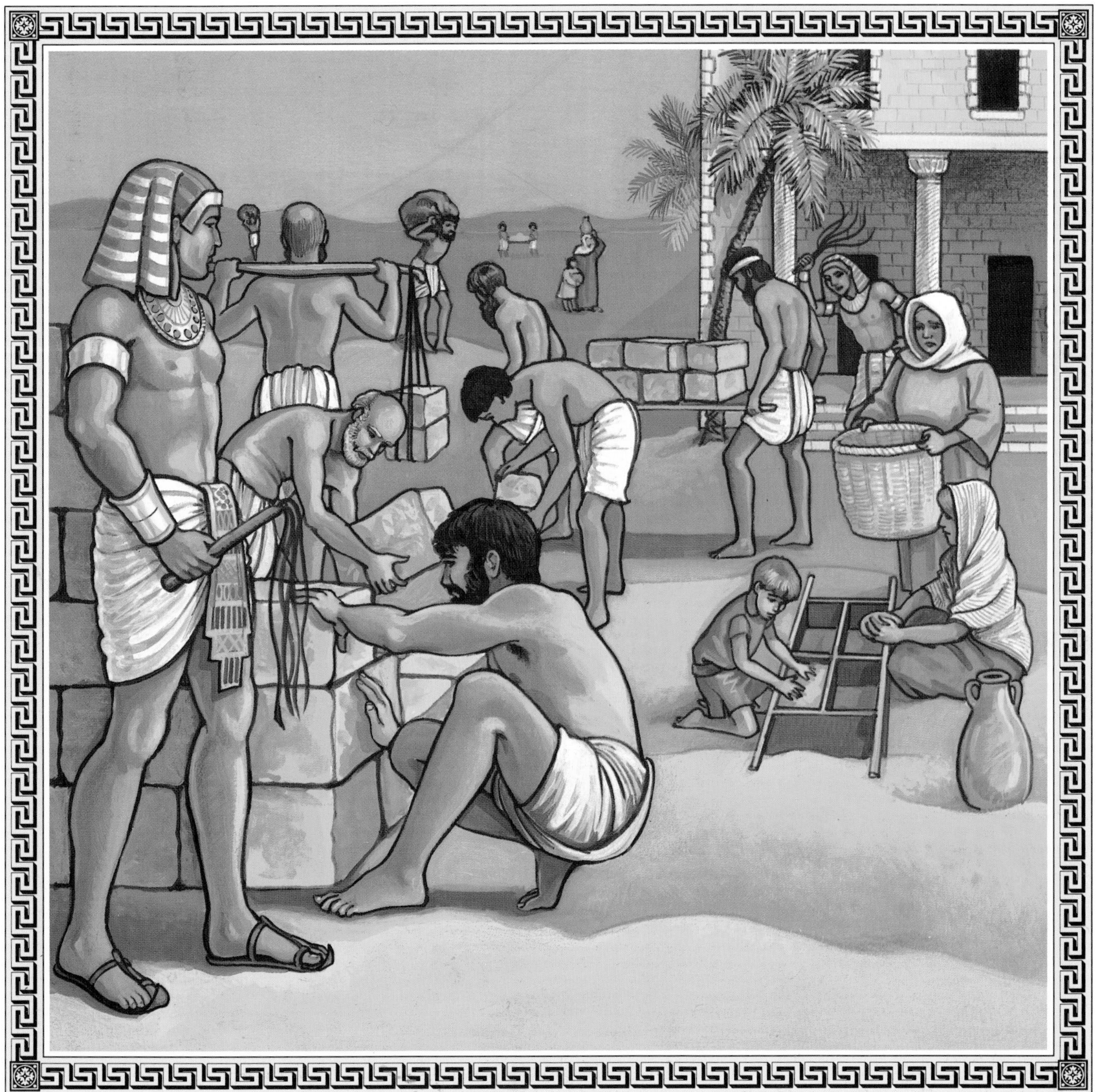

One day a beautiful baby boy was born into a young Israelite family. His mother and father hid the baby. They were afraid the Pharaoh's soldiers would find him and take him away. But the baby's mother had an idea.

"I am going to put him in a small straw boat in the river," she said. "The soldiers will never look there." The baby's sister Miriam stayed to keep watch over her little brother.

That very day, Pharaoh's daughter came to the river for a bath, and she saw the little straw boat!

"What is that basket in the water?" she asked her servants. When she opened the basket the baby was crying. The princess picked him up gently and held him. "Let's name him Moses," she said.

The princess looked at the baby's blanket and clothes. "Why, this is an Israelite child!" she exclaimed. "Let's find an Israelite nurse to take care of him."

At that moment, Miriam stepped out of her hiding place. "I'll find a nurse for you, princess," she said. Miriam rushed home and brought her mother to the river.

"Take this child and raise him for me," the princess told Moses' mother. "You must return him to me when he is grown."

Moses grew up with his family. When he was grown, he went to Pharaoh's palace to become the adopted son of Pharaoh's daughter. There, he learned to speak Egyptian, to be a soldier, and to lead the people. But in his heart, he loved God and never forgot his Israelite family and friends.

One day, Moses visited a city where Israelite slaves worked making bricks. It was hot and the slaves were exhausted. But a soldier kept beating them with a whip to make them work. This made Moses very angry and he told the soldier to stop. When the soldier refused, Moses fought him and killed him.

Pharaoh was furious that his adopted grandson had killed a soldier to defend Israelite slaves. Soldiers were hunting for Moses everywhere. So he ran far away from Egypt to the land of Midian. There, he wandered in the desert until he met the family of Jethro.

Jethro was a good man who also believed in God. Moses married one of Jethro's daughters, a young girl named Zipporah. Moses was happy in Midian. But in the meantime, his people in Egypt cried out to God for help, and God heard them.

Moses became a shepherd and took care of Jethro's flocks. One afternoon, when he was near a mountain called Mt. Sinai, he saw a bush that burned and burned, but it never burned up. Then a voice came from the bush.

"Moses, take off your sandals! This is holy ground!" it said. "I am God, the God of your people."

Moses was so afraid, he couldn't even look up. The Lord continued to speak, "I have heard my people cry out. And I am sending you to save them from Pharaoh. I have chosen a special land for them, a land filled with good things and much food. You will lead them there."

Moses was afraid of this great task, and he tried to make excuses. But God promised to help him.

Moses returned to Egypt and found his family. God had told him to ask his brother Aaron to help him lead the Israelites. Together with Aaron, Moses told the Israelites, "God will set you free."

The people were filled with joy. "Are you more powerful than Pharaoh?" they asked Moses. But Moses knew it was God's power that would free them.

Pharaoh laughed when Aaron and Moses came to him. "I don't care about your God," Pharaoh said. "Prove that he has power." So Moses and Aaron used the power of God to perform great wonders. They turned Aaron's staff into a snake; they turned river water into blood; they even filled Egypt with frogs, gnats, flies, and grasshoppers. They commanded thunderstorms and darkness. But still Pharaoh refused to let the Israelites go free.

Then God told Moses to warn Pharaoh one more time. "Let my people go or else the firstborn of every family will die this night." But Pharaoh's heart was as hard as stone.

Moses told the Israelites to pack everything up. "Tonight we leave," he said. "So make a special meal of lamb and bread and bitter spices to remind you of what God is doing for us." He also told them to mark their doors with the blood of a lamb.

Late that night, an angel came to Egypt. The angel did not stop at the houses with the mark of lamb's blood on the door. But in all the other houses, every firstborn died. Even Pharaoh's son died. The night was filled with loud cries, but the firstborn of Israel were safe. Because the angel passed over the Israelite homes, they called their meal "Passover."

Soon the Egyptians were begging the Israelites, "Leave us! Leave us before things get worse!" The Egyptians gave them gifts to try to make them go. And in the morning, the Israelites were set free.

Long caravans of animals and people followed Moses and Aaron as they left Egypt. Children skipped and the adults sang. The people had never been happier.

"We will be faithful to God forever," they said, "because he has saved us from the Egyptians."

During the day, God set a huge cloud in front of the Israelites for them to follow. During the night, a tower of fire led them onward.

Back in Egypt, Pharaoh changed his mind. "Why did we let those slaves escape?" he yelled at his soldiers. Pharaoh ran from his palace and jumped into his chariot. "Chase them! I will punish them for what their God did."

The Israelites were almost out of Egypt when they came to a huge lake. Scouts came to Moses saying, "Pharaoh and his army are coming! We're trapped!"

The people cried out in fear. But Moses told them to be quiet. "Do not be afraid. God will fight for you."

Moses turned toward the sea and raised his wooden staff in the air, as God told him to do. Suddenly, a great wind began to blow, and the sea opened, leaving a dry path to the other side. With a shout, the Israelites ran along the seabed to the other shore.

When the last of the Israelites had crossed the sea, everyone turned to look back. Six hundred Egyptian chariots were chasing them. Moses waited for the chariots to enter the pathway in the sea. Then God told him to raise his staff. When he did, the walls of water crashed down onto the Egyptians. God's people stood in amazement on the far shore.

"God has saved us," they said. "God has set us free." And that day they promised to believe in the Lord and follow Moses to the land that was promised to them.

THE STORY OF MOSES:

MOSES IN THE WILDERNESS

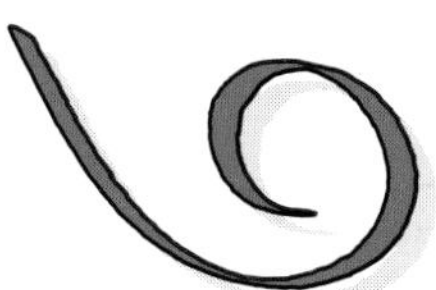

Moses and all the people of Israel stood in amazement. They had fled from slavery in Egypt. When Pharaoh had tried to catch them, God had opened a sea for them to pass through. Then God had closed it on the Egyptian army. The waters of the sea were still swirling wildly.

People started shouting. Moses and his sister Miriam sang, "Sing to the Lord! For he has won! He threw the horses and soldiers into the sea!"

Now the people knew that Moses was their true leader. "What will we do now?" they asked. "We are surrounded by desert. Where is this land God promised us?" Moses was sure that if the Lord could save them from Egypt he could also save them in the desert.

God told Moses to lead the people back to the mountain where he first met the Lord. Moses knew that his father-in-law Jethro would welcome him home again. But after three days of walking in the harsh desert, the people became thirsty.

"There's no water, Moses," they complained. "We will die in this desert. Are you lost?" Then they came to a small lake. The people rushed to drink the water, but they spit it out. It was bitter! But the Lord told Moses to toss a small tree into the water. Moses threw in the tree, and the water became sparkling and fresh.

Then God told the people, "If you follow me and love me and obey me, I will take care of you." Just to show what he meant, God led them to a place called Elim. It was beautiful! It had 12 bubbling springs and 70 palm trees. The people drank and swam and rested.

From Elim, Moses led the people through the desert for two more months. It was hot and dry, and there was nothing to eat. Soon they ran out of food, and again the people were angry at Moses.

"Did you bring us out here to die in the desert?" they cried. "Maybe we were better off as slaves in Egypt!" They forgot all about God's promises.

Moses prayed to God for help. One night the Lord sent wild birds from far away to settle in the Israelites' camp. The people caught them for food. And in the morning everyone found strange white wafers on the ground. They tasted like soft crackers with honey. The Israelites called this food "manna."

The birds came every night and the bread came every morning. "See," said Moses, "God is feeding you with bread that falls from heaven."

God took care of his people on their journey. He gave them water and protected them from their enemies. Every day God was with the Israelites, leading them through the desert.

At last, three months after leaving Egypt, Moses saw Jethro's home in the distance. Jethro ran out and hugged Moses. He showed the Israelites where to camp. Nearby, Moses could see the great mountain where God spoke to him.

After greeting Jethro and helping the people settle into their camp, Moses hiked to the top of the mountain. There God told him his plan. The many tribes of Israel camped at the bottom of the mountain and got ready to meet the Lord. Then God showed his power. Lightning and thunder shook the mountain. A dark cloud covered the top. The people watched this in wonder.

God wanted the Israelites to be his people forever. He loved them. God gave the people ten rules to live by. He wrote these rules on stone tablets and gave them to Moses. These are the Ten Commandments.

1. Love the Lord only and don't worship any other gods.

2. Do not build any statues of any gods and worship them.

3. Do not swear and use God's name foolishly.

4. Remember the Lord's Day. Make it holy because it belongs to God.

5. Respect your father and mother.

6. Do not murder.

7. Do not take someone else's husband or wife.

8. Do not steal.

9. Do not lie about other people.

10. Do not want what belongs to others.

The people promised to obey and love the Lord. They were happy that God had chosen them. But the Lord had much more to tell Moses. Moses climbed the mountain one day and did not return for weeks. The people thought, "Maybe Moses is dead. Maybe he left us. Maybe God has left too."

They turned to Aaron and asked him to build a new god for them. Aaron gathered up their gold jewelry, melted it, and made a golden calf. It reminded the people of the gods of Egypt. The people danced around it and sang songs for their new god. They forgot all about their promises to the Lord.

One night Moses came back. He was so angry that the people had broken their promise, he broke the stone tablets of the Ten Commandments. Then he crushed the calf into a fine powder.

When they saw Moses' anger, the Israelites were very sorry. They promised never to disobey again. God gave them a fresh start, too. He gave Moses new stone tablets and forgave the people. God loved his people, even though they sinned.

For almost two years the Israelites camped at Mount Sinai. They built a beautiful tent where God was worshiped. This was God's tent and when he was there a cloud rested over it. Inside were tables where people gave God gifts. A special chest deep inside held gifts from the Lord: the stone tablets, the staff that had worked wonders in Egypt, and a jar of manna.

The Israelites took the tent with them on their travels. God wanted the people to know that he liked being with them, going where they went, because he was their friend as well as their powerful Lord.

Soon it was time to leave. Everyone was ready to enter the land God had promised them. When they were close, Moses sent 12 spies into the land.

"The promised land is beautiful," ten of the spies reported. "But the people who live there now are strong. We will never get in." But two of the spies, Caleb and Joshua, disagreed. They said God was stronger than their enemies.

The people were afraid. "It was better being slaves in Egypt than following God in this desert," they cried.

The Lord was very angry. "Because you won't believe me," he said, "Israel will wander in the desert for 40 years. Joshua, Caleb, and your children will enter my promised land, but not you." And so the Lord turned the Israelites away from the wonderful land, back into the harsh desert.

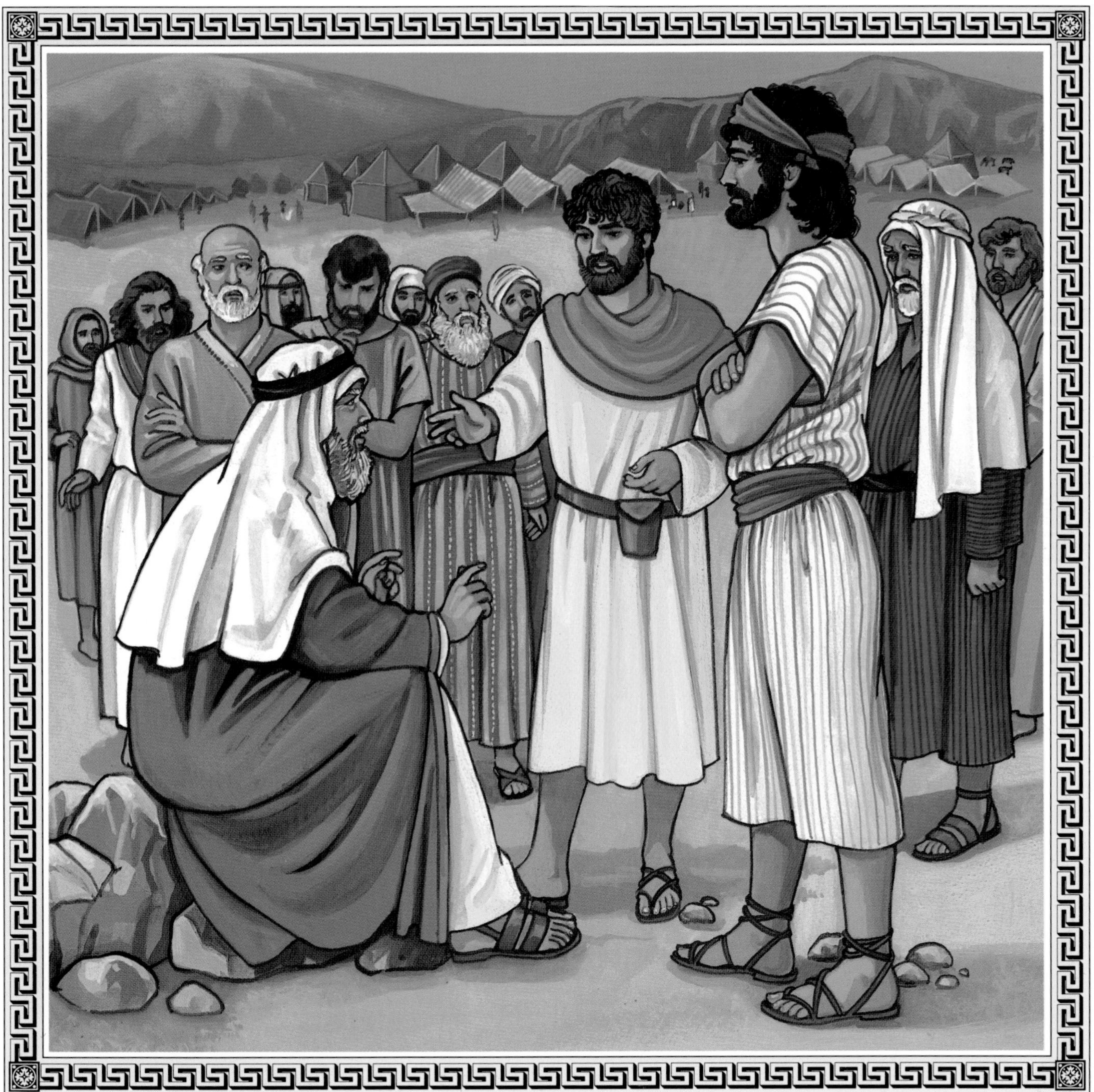

Life in the desert was very hard. Everyone lived in tents and walked for miles looking for water and good camps. But God did not forget his people. He gave them manna every morning and sent birds every night. But still the people argued with Moses. They did not want to obey and follow the Lord.

Once they were attacked by poisonous snakes because they were complaining so much. The Lord told Moses to make a bronze snake and put it on a tall pole. Then Moses told the people, "If you look at this snake and trust God, he will save you." Everyone who obeyed Moses lived.

After many years, Moses led the people to the area near the Jordan River. Everyone knew that on the other side of the river was God's holy land. This time, they remembered to obey God and to trust his power.

Moses died in this place, and Joshua became Israel's new leader. Like Moses, Joshua loved God, and God's power helped him. When the Israelites wanted to cross the Jordan River, God stopped its flow and a dry path opened before them! It was just like the miracle of Moses when they left Egypt!

The Israelites settled in the land God had promised them, and they lived there for many years. And God was always with them even when they were afraid.

SAMSON AND DELILAH

A long time ago in Israel, God's people refused to follow him. Because the people had turned their backs on God, he stopped protecting them from their enemies.

Near Israel lived a people called the Philistines. They were sworn enemies of the Israelites. Often, the Philistines would attack Israel, stealing and destroying homes, crops, and animals. When God stopped protecting the Israelites, the Philistines conquered Israel. Then the people of Israel cried out to God for help.

Manoah and his wife were Israelites who lived during the time of these great troubles. One year, God sent an angel to visit the couple. The angel told them that they would have a son who would rescue their people from their enemies. This son would be a mighty warrior of God.

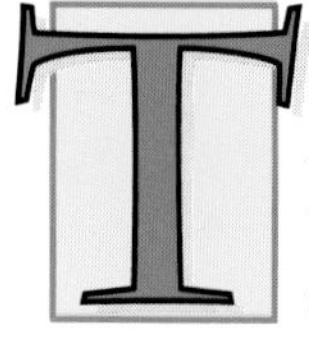

he angel explained that this child would be different than any other boy in all of Israel.

"He will defeat the Philistines in war," the angel said, "and drive them from your land. His strength and courage will make him famous. He will also promise to keep his whole life close to God. To show his special promise to God, the boy must never cut his hair."

Soon Manoah's wife gave birth to a baby boy, just as the angel had predicted. They named him Samson. He quickly grew into a strong and handsome young man. His hair grew long and thick, reminding everyone that God's power was in him. But some people wondered if this power was too much for Samson. Sometimes he seemed to love this power more than he loved God.

hen Samson was grown, he fell in love with a Philistine woman from the town of Timnah.

Manoah was shocked. "God's people do not marry Philistines," he told his son. "The Philistines don't follow God." But Samson insisted that Manoah talk to the woman's parents.

On the road to Timnah, Samson was attacked by a fierce lion. The young man killed the lion with his bare hands, but he did not tell anyone about this.

After they talked with the woman's family, Samson and his parents went back home. Some time later, Samson returned to Timnah to marry the girl. When he passed the body of the lion he saw that honeybees had built a hive in its belly. He took some of the honey and ate it. But he told no one where it came from.

The wedding feast was crowded and noisy. Everyone wanted to see the famous Israelite who was marrying a Philistine woman! For seven days the guests ate, drank, sang, and danced. But Samson wanted to make the party even more fun. He decided to play a game with the Philistines.

Samson called some Philistines to gather around him. "If you can guess the answer to my riddle, I will give each of you a beautiful robe," he declared. The people listened carefully.

"Out of the eater came something to eat. Out of the strong came something sweet." Samson looked around. "What am I talking about?" he grinned. For days, everyone was puzzled. Some of the Philistines whispered to Samson's new wife that she should get the answer out of him.

For many days, Samson's young wife begged him for the answer. At last, on the final day of the wedding feast, Samson gave in. She ran to her friends and told them the answer.

"What is sweeter than honey, Samson? What is stronger than a lion?" they jeered. Samson was so angry he could barely control himself.

"If you had not used my wife, I would be the winner!" he shouted. In a fury, Samson ran away from the wedding. He fought with Philistines in all the towns he came across and killed many people. Because of this, the Philistines hated Samson.

For a long time, Samson did not return to his wife, and so she went back to her family. Because she was alone, her father said she could marry another man.

A long time later, Samson did return in search of his wife. He was angrier than ever when he learned that she was now married to someone else!

Samson lost his temper again. He caught 300 foxes. Then he divided them in pairs and tied a burning torch between their tails. The foxes ran away through the Philistines' fields. In the blazing flames, the crops and trees burned until nothing was left.

Samson killed so many Philistines that his own people started to worry. So when an army of Israelites found him, they tied him with two ropes and gave him to the Philistines. Samson tore the ropes apart as if they were sewing threads. He found the jawbone of a donkey and used it to kill a thousand Philistine soldiers. No one in the entire land was as strong as Samson.

Later, Samson fell in love with another Philistine woman named Delilah. When the Philistine leaders heard about this, they spoke to her in secret. They offered to pay her 1,100 silver coins if she would reveal the secret of Samson's power. She agreed.

"Samson, my love, tell me how your power can be stopped," she said one night.

"If they tie me with seven fresh bow strings, I cannot get out," he said. That night, as Samson slept, Delilah did just that. But when the Philistine soldiers came to grab him, he easily broke the strings and slipped away.

The next night, Delilah asked him again for his secret. "If they tie me with new ropes, I will be caught," he said. After he went to sleep Delilah tied him up, but when the Philistines came, he again broke free and escaped.

When Samson returned to Delilah, she asked him again. "Samson, tell me no more lies. How can you be defeated?" Samson told her if someone wove seven locks of his hair into a loom, he would have no power. Delilah did this and the Philistines attacked, but once again Samson escaped easily.

"Samson, if you love me you will tell me your secret," Delilah finally said. And Samson told her the truth.

"If you cut off my hair, then I will be weak." That night, as Samson slept, Delilah called in a barber to cut Samson's hair. This time, when Philistines rushed into the house, Samson's power was gone! When his hair was cut, God's power left him.

The Philistines blinded him, put him in chains, and threw him in prison.

Samson suffered terribly in prison. The Philistines made him work hard and gave him little to eat. But nobody noticed that Samson's hair was starting to grow back.

One night, a large group of Philistines decided to have a party. They brought Samson from the prison so that they could mock him. Samson prayed to God as he had never prayed before. He prayed to have his great strength back just one more time. He reached out and grabbed two huge pillars that held up the house. Samson gave a great cry, "Let me die with the Philistines!" Then he pushed against the pillars with all his might.

The power of God returned to Samson. The entire house came crashing down and many, many Philistines died with him that day.

God had given Samson a great gift, his wonderful strength. His long, flowing hair stood for his power and his promise to God. But Samson came to love his power more than he loved God. When his hair was cut, Samson learned a terrible lesson. He learned that his strength came from God and that God is stronger than even the mightiest of people.

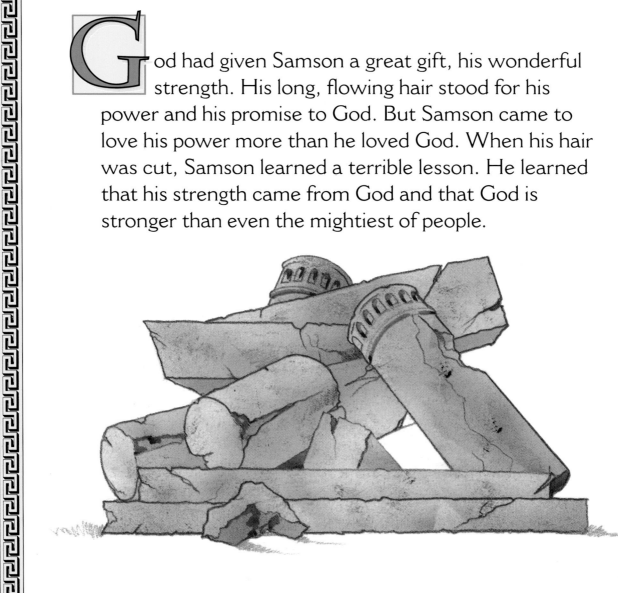

DAVID AND GOLIATH

Long ago in the town of Bethlehem, there lived a boy named David. He was a handsome young shepherd boy. More important than how he looked on the outside, David was beautiful on the inside. God knew this and watched over him.

David and his eight brothers were all sons of Jesse. Every day when David went to tend the sheep, he would grab his shepherd's staff and harp. With a quick wave to his father, David would be off to watch the sheep. He would play the harp to calm the sheep and help make the day go by faster.

Nearby in Bethlehem lived Saul, the king of Israel. Saul was an unhappy man. At one time he had loved and respected God. But then one day Saul displeased God. After that, Saul became very sad.

One day when Saul felt sad, a servant suggested that they find someone to play the harp for him. The music might make the king feel better. Saul thought it was a good idea. Another servant knew David and suggested he play for the king.

They asked Jesse, David's father, if he would allow David to play for the king. He agreed, and David went to the palace.

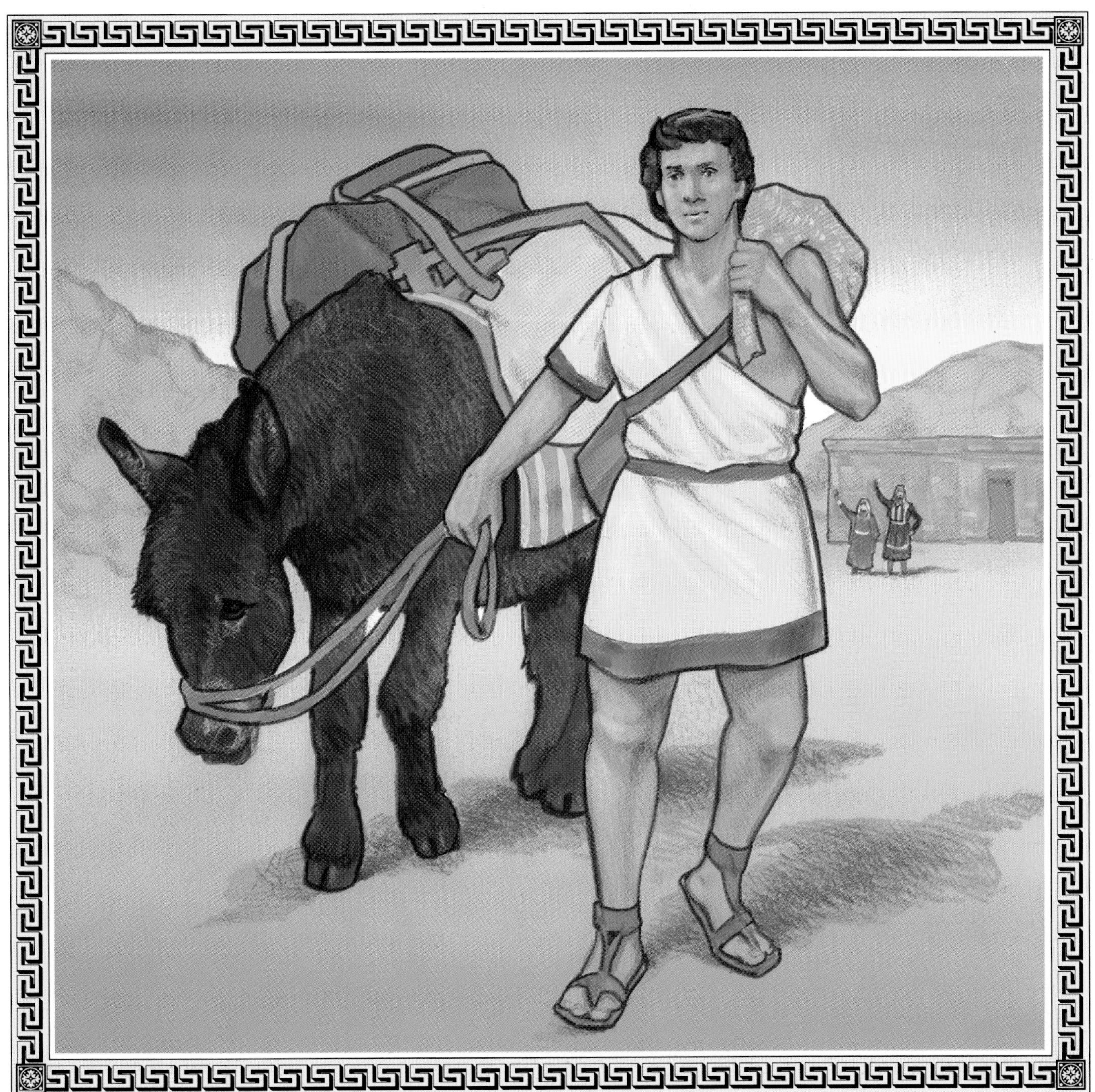

David's music did make King Saul feel better. Saul wanted him to stay at the palace. So he asked Jesse, "Will you let David stay with me? He pleases me very much."

Meanwhile, David's brothers joined Saul's army. Since they were gone, David had to travel back and forth, playing his harp at the palace and tending the sheep at home. On one trip home, Jesse said, "I hear the Philistines are ready to fight. I am worried about your older brothers. Take this food to them. Then come back and let me know how they are."

David got up early the next day, picked up the sack of food, and started on the trip.

As David got near to the camp, he heard yelling. The two armies were lined up and ready to fight. He left the sack of food with a guard and went to find his brothers. As David greeted them he heard:

"Today I dare the army of Israel." It was a giant Philistine soldier trying to make someone fight him. "Give me a man to fight. If he should win, we are your servants. If I win, you are our servants."

Saul's soldiers were afraid. This man was so big and strong. Surely no one could win a fight against him. David stepped right up and shouted, "I will fight the giant Goliath myself!"

David's brothers told him to be quiet and go home. But David would not listen. He repeated his promise to a soldier who then told King Saul. The king sent for David. "Don't be afraid," insisted David. "I will go and fight this Philistine."

"You are just a boy who tends sheep," said the king. "Goliath has been a warrior since he was a child."

"I know I am a shepherd boy," admitted David. But he told the king how he had rescued sheep from bears and lions. He wasn't afraid then and he wasn't afraid now. "God has saved me from both lions and bears," David told Saul. "God will save me from Goliath, too."

King Saul knew what had to be done. "Go and may God be with you!" the king said. Saul wanted to help David, so he had heavy armor put on him. But David was not used to it. "I cannot walk with this armor," he told Saul. "It is too heavy."

David removed the armor. Walking to a nearby stream, he picked out five smooth stones. He put them in his pouch, grabbed his sling and shepherd's crook, and started off to fight the giant.

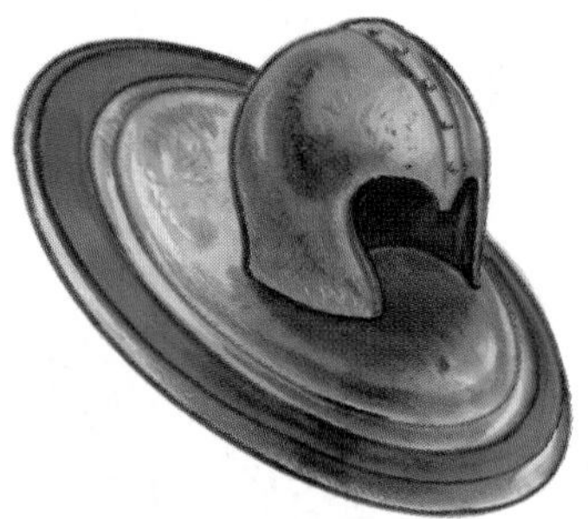

Goliath marched his huge body toward David. The sunshine glared off the large shiny helmet on the giant's head. His body was protected by heavy armor. Layers of armor covered his legs. And in Goliath's hand was a fierce-looking spear that weighed over 15 pounds! The giant was truly a frightening sight.

Goliath stomped closer to David. He looked down at the creature far beneath him. He thought David was much too young and small. Was someone playing a joke on him?

"Am I a dog that you come to me with sticks?" yelled the angry Philistine. "Come to me and I will feed you to the birds and wild animals."

David answered Goliath, "You come at me with a sword and spear. But I come to you in the name of God who protects the army of Israel whom you dared."

David continued, "This very day I will strike you down. Everyone will know that there is a God in Israel. And that God does not save by spear and by sword."

The angry Philistine ran at David to attack him. David raced toward the battle line to meet the giant. As he went, David pulled a stone from his bag. Then he stopped, fixed the stone in his sling, and flung it mightily toward the Philistine. The stone flew through the air toward the vicious giant.

The stone struck the giant on his forehead. Goliath fell face down on the ground. The earth trembled from his weight. David ran and stood over Goliath. He grabbed the giant's sword from its case. He held the sword high to show both armies he won.

The Philistines saw that Goliath, their champion, was no more. How could even the mightiest giant try to defeat someone when God was on their side? Realizing there was no hope, they ran away with Saul's army right behind them.

David went back to Saul's tent to tell him about Goliath. When the king heard the good news, he was so happy! He knew that God was with David.

Saul thanked David for saving Israel. Saul's son, Jonathan, gave David robes and armor. David lived in the palace like a royal son.

David still played his harp for the king. But Saul made the boy a leader in his army. David won battle after battle. The people grew to know and love him. David later became king. With God's help, he won many more battles against the Philistines.

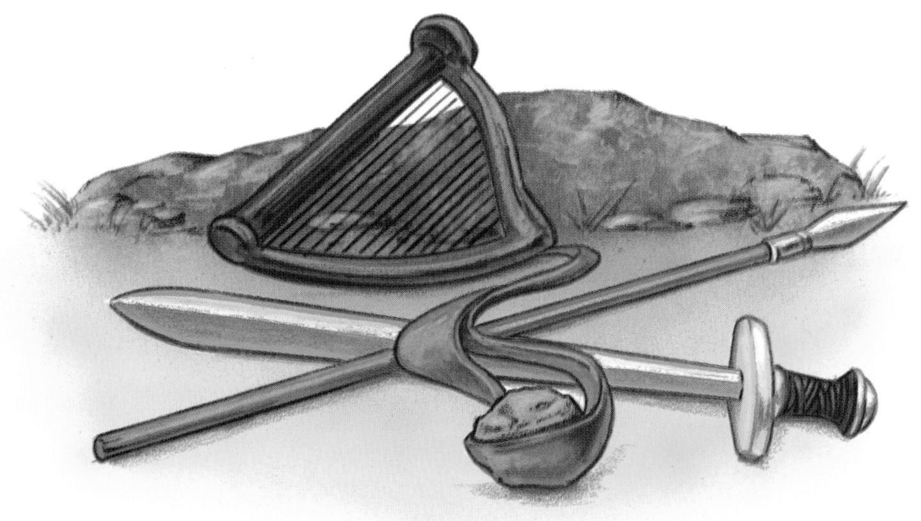

The Story of Solomon

"Who will be king after David dies?" Now that King David was very old, the question was on everyone's lips. The king of Israel had many sons.

In those days, the king could have more than one wife. Bathsheba was King David's favorite wife. One day when David was in bed and feeling very ill, she went to him. Bathsheba said, "My lord, you promised that our son Solomon would be the next king. Have you forgotten?"

Nathan the prophet also came in and spoke. "All the people are watching you, David. Choose your king or your sons will fight!"

Outside the palace, crowds were already cheering for one of David's other sons, Adonijah. They thought he would be the next king.

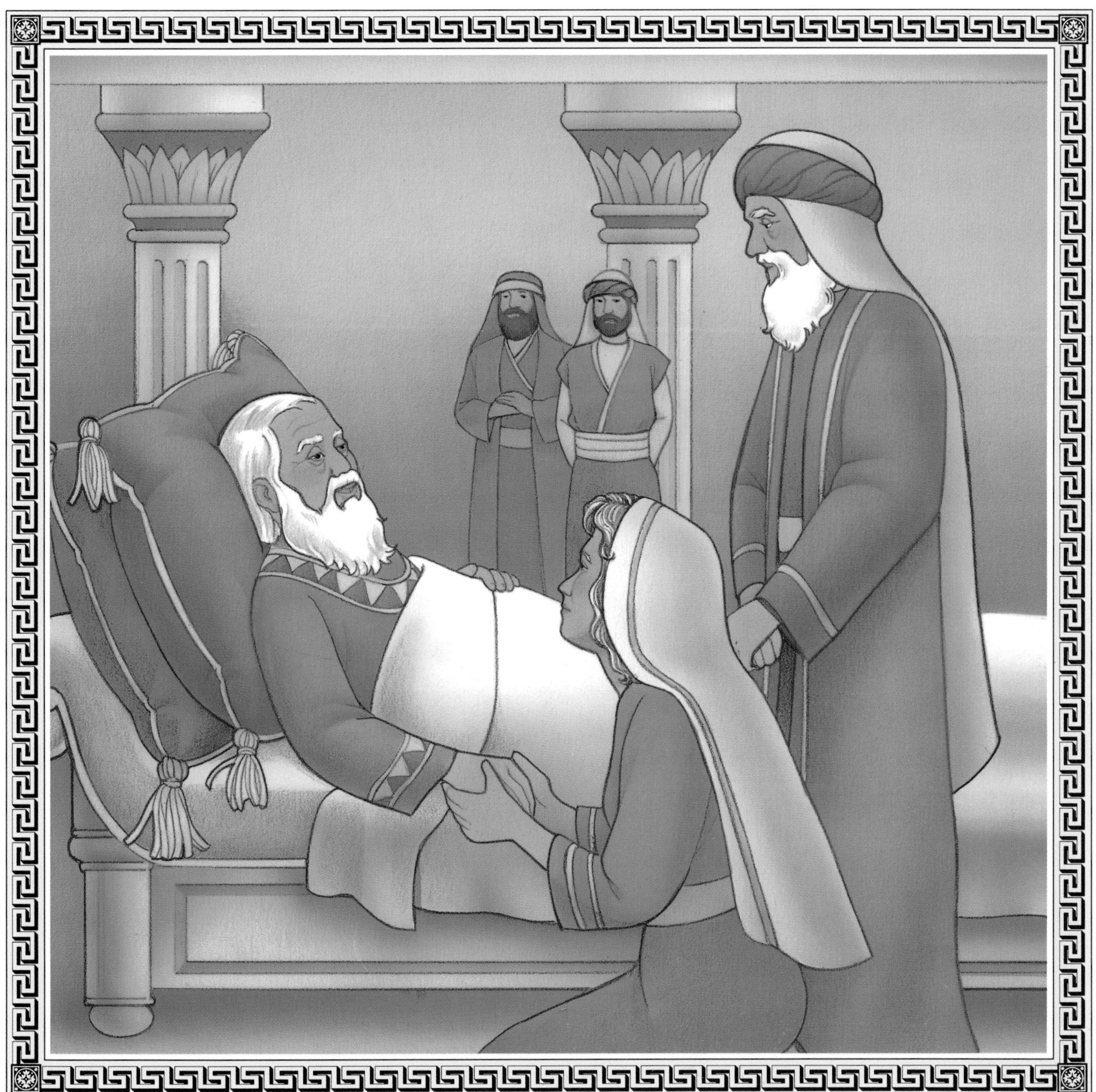

King David leaned up on one elbow and said, "Bring me the priest Zadok! He will speak for God!" When Zadok arrived, David announced, "Solomon my son will be king after me! Now take him down to the spring of Gihon and put the crown on him. Tell all the people that this is my will."

Zadok and Solomon rode to Gihon together. At the spring, Zadok poured a special oil on Solomon's head to show that God's spirit was on him.

"Long live King Solomon!" the crowd shouted.

Solomon's brother Adonijah was frightened because he had tried to be king. He ran and hid, but Solomon had him found. Adonijah begged Solomon not to kill him. But Solomon was not angry. He lifted his brother to his feet and told him to return home in peace.

When King David knew that he was going to die, he called Solomon to his side. "I am about to go and be with the Lord," he said in a tired voice. "You must be brave and strong. You must be faithful to God and remember all of his laws. Obey him with all your heart and soul. If you do this, you will be a great king."

The old king rested for a moment and then went on, "Be fair to the people. Forgive others and be loyal to your friends. When people are wicked, you must punish them, but always be fair in your punishments."

Then King David died. There was great sadness in Jerusalem and throughout the land. David had been a courageous leader and a man of God.

One night when King Solomon was in bed sleeping, the Lord came to him in a dream. "Ask what you want and it will be yours," he said. Solomon knew that he would not be great unless God helped him.

"Lord," he replied, "please give me wisdom. Help me to know the difference between good and evil. Show me how to lead your people."

God was very pleased. "You have spoken well," he said. "You have not asked for money or great armies for yourself. You will have greater wisdom than any other person. And I will give you even more than that. You will have riches and power like no other king in Israel. If you follow me, I will give you a long life."

Solomon woke up with a joyful feeling. He knew that God had spoken to him in the dream.

Soon, two women tested the king's wisdom. "This baby is mine!" one yelled. "No! He's mine!" screamed the other.

The women explained their story. Both women had just had a baby. The first woman said that the second woman's baby had died in the night. The second woman had then secretly taken the first woman's baby. The second woman swore that the first was lying and that the baby was hers. How could a king decide which woman was the real mother?

When the king stood up, everyone in the room was silent. Solomon had made up his mind.

"Bring me a sword," he said. As a servant rushed out, people whispered nervously to each other. Why did he want a sword? Would he kill the baby?

King Solomon spoke again. "Since each woman wants the baby, I have decided to cut him in half. Each of you may have half of the baby!" The people were shocked! How could Solomon do such a terrible thing? The room went silent.

One servant held the baby in the air, and Solomon ordered another to lift his sword. Suddenly, the first woman cried out, "Stop! Give the baby to her. At least then my baby will live."

Solomon ordered the servant to set the sword on the floor. It was all a trick. Solomon had never planned to kill the baby. "Give the child to the first woman. A true mother loves her child so much she would even give it up to save it!"

Everyone left that day amazed at the wisdom God had given King Solomon.

Solomon became famous throughout the land. Kings from other countries visited Israel to meet this new ruler. Solomon made friends with them and traded with them to make his kingdom richer. Solomon was also famous for wise sayings called proverbs. The Bible contains many proverbs like these:

"The fear of the Lord is the beginning of knowledge; fools despise wisdom and teaching."

"Trust in the Lord with all your heart, and do not rely on your own thoughts. In all your ways follow him, and he will make your path straight."

"My child, obey and never forget your father and mother's teachings. Tie them to your heart! Wear them around your neck! When you walk they will lead you. When you sleep, they will watch over you."

Solomon's father David had always wanted to build a great temple for the Lord, but God would not let him. God said Solomon should build the temple. So Solomon made preparations to start the building. This place would be God's house, so it had to be the most beautiful building in all Jerusalem.

Everyone in Israel was excited about the job. Every man worked on it in shifts for a month at a time. Solomon sent 30,000 men to Lebanon to cut trees. He sent 80,000 men to cut stone and 70,000 to carry things. Precious gifts of gold, jewels, and rare woods came from faraway kings. Craftsmen worked and worked for seven years until the Temple stood out as a gleaming golden jewel in the heart of Jerusalem.

Solomon also wanted to build a splendid palace for himself. After all, he was the king, and a king needed a house of beauty. He used more builders to cut more stone and trees. And soon his palace was standing in Jerusalem, just as high as God's temple.

But everyone noticed one thing: Solomon's palace was larger than God's temple. And Solomon worked thirteen years on his palace, nearly twice as long as he worked on God's house.

Solomon wanted more power and more riches. He asked the daughters of other kings to marry him, and soon he had 700 wives. He let them worship other gods around Jerusalem just to keep them happy. Some of the wives were evil but Solomon kept them anyway, so that their fathers would be Solomon's friends.

At the end of his life, Solomon disappointed God. He cared more about his wives and their gods than about God and his people. Because of this, God decreed that after Solomon's death there would be war in Israel. The country would be split in two.

God had given Solomon more wisdom than any other king, and Solomon had done much good for his people. But because he turned away from God, the people of Israel suffered for many years.

THE STORY OF ESTHER

In the ancient land of Persia, there was a king named Ahasuerus. He was searching for a beautiful young woman to be his queen. The loveliest women from every city were brought to the palace. The king was to choose his queen from among them. Each would be presented to the king, and the one who pleased him would become the new queen.

Esther came to the palace filled with excitement. Would she be chosen? Her family was not rich or famous. Her parents had died and she lived with her older cousin Mordecai. Esther was Jewish, but she kept her faith a secret because she thought the king might not want a Jewish queen.

Esther was not only beautiful, she was also very wise. And when she came to the king, he loved her most of all. Soon Esther was wearing the queen's golden crown.

One day, when Mordecai was out walking in the city, he decided to rest on a bench just outside the palace gate. He could hear two soldiers talking nearby. Suddenly he realized that the men were planning to kill the king! They and their friends wanted to take over the palace and make themselves kings.

Mordecai secretly slipped into the palace and told a servant to find the young queen at once. Mordecai then told her everything he had heard.

Esther warned the king about the plot and told him how Mordecai had saved him. King Ahasuerus was very upset. He arrested the men at the gate and found their friends. But he forgot all about Mordecai. One of the king's servants wrote the whole story down in a book so that the king could remember it later.

Haman was the man King Ahasuerus trusted most of all. He helped the king make important decisions. But in his heart, Haman was evil and vain. He wanted the people to bow down before him, as if he were a king. He even got the king to issue an order that people must do just that.

One day when Haman was walking near the city gate, he saw that everyone was bowing except Mordecai. Mordecai's faith taught him to bow down only to God.

"Why aren't you bowing down to me?" Haman demanded angrily. But Mordecai stood firm.

Haman learned that Mordecai was Jewish. He went to the king and convinced him that all of the Jews in Persia should be killed and their homes taken. This would happen in 12 months.

Throughout Persia, Jewish families cried out to God and prayed for help. Everyone was very afraid.

Esther was worried, too. No one knew she was Jewish and no one knew that Mordecai was her cousin. What would the king say if he found out that Esther was Jewish? Would she also be killed?

Mordecai called for Esther late one night and they talked in secret. "You must help your people, Esther," he said. "You must speak to the king for us and save your people. Who knows? Maybe you have become queen for this very reason."

Esther was even more frightened now. The queen could only visit the king if he invited her. If she entered the king's rooms without his invitation, he could decide to have her killed!

Esther realized that she would need all her courage. She told Mordecai to ask the Jews to not eat or drink, but only to pray for her, for three days. Esther did the same. Then she put on her finest royal robe and went in to see King Ahasuerus.

Would he smile? Would he greet her? Would he punish her for coming without an invitation? Esther stepped slowly into the king's chamber. She was so afraid she didn't know if she would even be able to speak. But when King Ahasuerus saw her he held out his hand. She was safe!

"What is your request, my queen?" he asked. "You can have anything you want."

Esther answered, "I would like you and Haman to join me tonight at a special banquet."

The banquet was wonderful and the king was pleased. "Now what is your request? As I said, you may have anything you want," he said.

"I ask that you come to another banquet tomorrow," Esther answered. King Ahasuerus happily agreed.

Haman left the banquet feeling very proud. "Imagine a banquet just for me and the king," he thought. "And tomorrow the same!" He and his wife laughed all evening at their good fortune. "No one is closer to the king than me," he bragged.

But still he thought about the Jewish people he did not like. He thought about people who were not afraid of him, and Mordecai came to mind. Haman's hatred burned against him. So Haman decided that day to kill Mordecai. He would have him hanged in public.

The night after the first banquet, King Ahasuerus could not sleep. He called his servant and said, "Read to me the story of what I have done as king."

The servant began to read, and soon he came to the story of how Mordecai had saved the king. "Wait! We never did do anything to honor this Mordecai," said Ahasuerus. Now Haman just happened to be waiting outside the king's chamber to tell him that he wanted to put Mordecai to death. But instead the king ordered him, "Find Mordecai! Give him one of my best horses and finest robes! Walk him through the streets! And tell everyone that this is how a king honors a friend."

Haman was stunned. His enemy was now the king's friend. He was embarrassed and furious as he led Mordecai through the streets.

The next day King Ahasuerus and Haman attended Queen Esther's banquet again. More food, more wine, and more music filled the palace halls. When the king was happy and full he asked Esther what she wanted.

"Great king, someone is trying to destroy my people. He is taking our homes, selling our children into slavery, and hurting your kingdom." The king still did not know that Esther was Jewish.

"Who is this man?" demanded the king. Esther pointed to Haman and said, "This is our enemy, the wicked Haman!"

The king's anger was like a thunderstorm. "What Haman planned for Mordecai I will now do to Haman," he announced.

The king had Haman hanged just as Haman had planned to hang Mordecai. On the same day, King Ahasuerus called for Mordecai. He ordered his servants to give Mordecai the robes and rings of Haman.

"From now on you will serve me as a trusted servant," he declared. "You will take Haman's place at my side." The king was so happy with Esther that he gave her all of Haman's wealth as well as his home.

But Queen Esther still worried. "What if other people far away try to carry out Haman's plan to kill God's people?" she asked. So the king wrote a special letter to all governors of the land. It said that Haman's words about the Jews were wrong. And if anyone hurt them, the Jews were free to fight back against their enemies.

When the day came, the Jews did fight back, because there were still some people in Persia who wanted to harm them. But for many years after that, the Jewish people were safe and enjoyed a special place in the land.

To this day, Jewish people celebrate this great rescue. During the festival of Purim they remember the way Esther saved her people through her courage and faith.

Daniel in the Lions' Den

Long ago in the city of Jerusalem, there lived a young boy named Daniel. Jerusalem had been taken over by a king named Nebuchadnezzar. The king said that the people of Jerusalem must follow his laws now.

The king said, "Jerusalem is mine! I order my soldiers to bring all the best royal and noble sons of Jerusalem to my palace in Babylon." King Nebuchadnezzar wanted to train them to work in his court.

Daniel and his three friends were chosen by the soldiers, along with other boys, to come live at the palace in Babylon. This is how Daniel came to live in Babylon.

The king put his palace master in charge of the boys. He was to make sure the boys were well taken care of and that they went to school. The boys studied what pleased the king.

Daniel and his friends learned more than anyone else. God watched over them and gave them wisdom beyond their years. God gave Daniel the special gift of understanding dreams.

Daniel's friends were given special jobs in the kingdom. Daniel stayed in the palace. He became known as someone who had the spirit of God. Daniel explained what no other person could explain. He served King Nebuchadnezzar and every king after him.

Years later, King Belshazzar had a party. During the party a huge hand appeared and made strange writing on the wall. The king did not understand what it meant. Someone told the king that Daniel might be able to explain it.

The king had Daniel look at the writing. Daniel told him, "You rebelled against the Lord of heaven. You worshiped other gods. You thought they were better than he is." The king thanked Daniel and gave him a very important job in the kingdom.

The next king, named Darius, planned to give Daniel an even more important job. This made some of the other workers angry.

These other men tried to find something to make Daniel look bad. But he had done nothing wrong. They needed a plan. They were going to trick the king!

They went to King Darius and said, "We think that you should make a law that people can pray only to you for the next thirty days. If they pray to anyone else, they will be thrown to the lions."

"That would be nice," thought the king. He signed the paper. He did not realize what the evil men were planning.

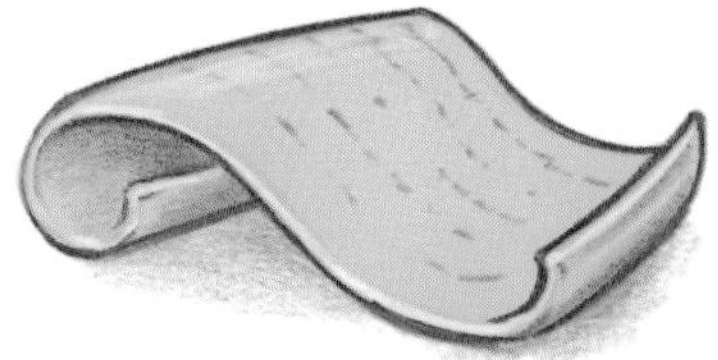

Daniel heard about the law. But since he was a faithful servant of the Lord, he continued to pray to God. He would kneel down in front of the open window upstairs and pray.

The evil men saw him praying. They knew their plan had worked. Quickly, they ran back to King Darius. They said, "Didn't you sign a law that said no person should pray to anyone except to you?" "That's correct," answered the king. "Otherwise, they will be thrown in the lions' den."

"Daniel doesn't listen to you," the men reported. "He continues to pray to God. He must be punished as you said."

King Darius could not believe what had happened! He had never meant to hurt Daniel. He tried and tried to find a way to save Daniel. But a law signed by the king could not be changed, even by the king. There was nothing he could do.

The guards got ready to throw Daniel into the den of lions. King Darius wanted to talk to Daniel. He went to Daniel and said, "May your God, whom you faithfully serve, keep you safe."

The king and his officials put their royal clay stamps in the rock that covered the opening. That way they would know no one had tried to let Daniel out of the den. Sadly, the king went back to his palace.

King Darius was so sad. He could not eat. He could not sleep. All night long he thought of poor Daniel. He went outside early the next morning and ran to the den. "Daniel," he called out, "are you hurt? Did your God protect you?"

"Yes, king," answered Daniel, "God sent an angel to shut the mouths of the lions. I have not been harmed." The king was so happy! Daniel was alive and well! God had saved him!

King Darius could not wait to see Daniel. He just had to see for himself that Daniel was not hurt. The king ordered his guards to take Daniel out of the lions' den. Many men came to remove the stone from the opening. The royal seal was still there. They lifted Daniel out of the den.

King Darius greeted Daniel warmly. Then he made sure he was unharmed. "I'm so glad you are not harmed," said the king. "Your God protected you."

King Darius went back to his palace. "Guards!" cried out the king. "Bring me the evil men who tricked me and tried to harm my faithful servant Daniel."

One by one, the evil men were brought in front of the king. King Darius was very unhappy with them. He decided that the men should have the same punishment they tricked him into giving Daniel.

Then King Darius wrote to all people throughout his empire: "All the people in my kingdom should obey Daniel's God. This is the God who lives forever. This God saves people. Daniel was saved from the lions."

From that day on, Daniel and his friends lived in peace in the kingdom of King Darius.

Jonah and the Whale

The people who lived in Nineveh were making God very unhappy. They had forgotten about God and what he wanted them to do. God wanted to send a message to the people. He chose Jonah, an Israelite, to be his messenger.

God said to Jonah, "Go to the city of Nineveh. Tell the people they have made me angry with their wicked ways. Tell them I will punish them."

The idea of doing this made Jonah afraid. He knew he had heard the voice of God. Yet, he didn't want to make the long trip to Nineveh. He was frightened because the people there were enemies of the people of Israel.

Rather than doing as God had asked, Jonah decided to hide. "I must find a place where God won't find me," Jonah thought. He packed some food and money and started out for Joppa. Joppa was a busy city in the opposite direction from Nineveh. Jonah hoped he could hide among the people of Joppa.

When he reached the bustling city, he became afraid again. "God will find me here and punish me," he worried. "I must go farther away." Jonah thought and thought about where to go. Then he noticed a ship.

"I know what I must do," he said. "I will take this ship across the sea to Tarshish. Surely, God will not find me there."

Jonah payed for his ticket and got on the ship. Tired from the long journey, Jonah went down into the cabin of the ship. He found a comfortable place to lay down and fell asleep. A short time later, the captain ordered the ship to leave the harbor. He looked at the blue sky overhead. The day was perfect for sailing.

Once they were out to sea, however, the sky changed greatly. A large storm swept over the sea. A strong wind rocked the boat. The rolling sea threatened to break the ship apart. The sailors were afraid. They threw the ship's cargo into the sea. They hoped a lighter ship would make it through the storm.

The danger did not go away. Each man prayed to his god. In spite of their prayers, the raging storm continued. The captain rushed to Jonah. "Get up," he ordered. "What are you doing asleep? Call on your God. Perhaps your God will keep us from dying."

The sailors above shouted to one another. "Someone has brought this storm upon us." They decided to cast lots (which was like drawing straws) to see who was causing all the problems.

When they cast the lots, it became clear that Jonah was responsible for all the trouble they were having. Everyone had questions for him.

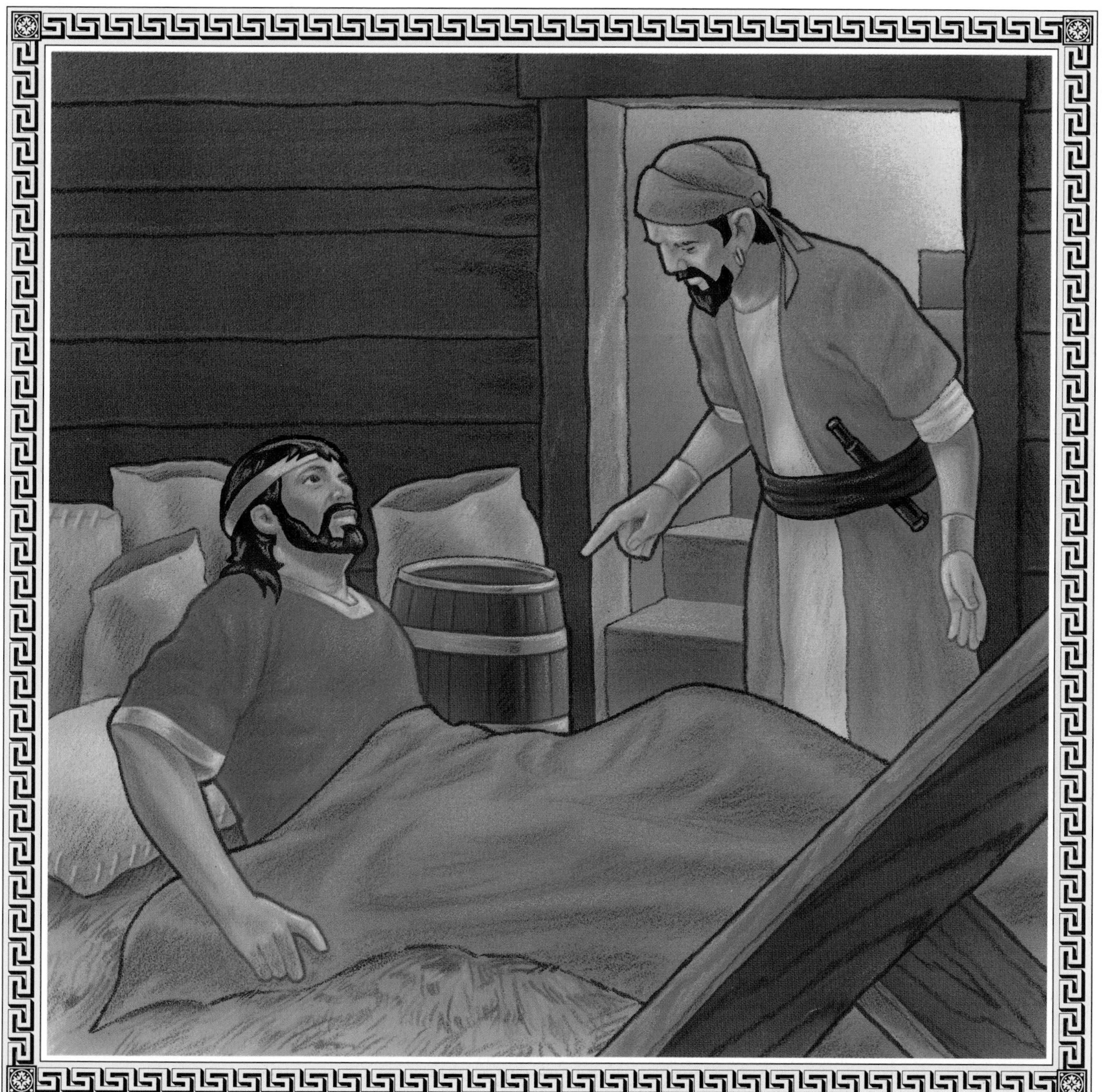

"Why did you bring this storm?" asked the captain. "Where are you from? Who are your people?" Jonah answered, "I am a Hebrew from the land of Israel." Then Jonah explained that he was running away from God. The men were even more afraid. "What shall we do to quiet the sea?"

Jonah now realized there was nowhere to hide from God. So he told the sailors to throw him into the sea. "Then the sea will quiet down for you," he said.

The sailors didn't want to throw Jonah overboard. So they tried everything to bring the ship back to land. But the winds were too strong. Finally, they picked Jonah up and threw him into the sea.

At once, the winds stopped blowing. The sea stopped raging. The sky brightened. The sailors thought of Jonah and thanked God for their safety.

But Jonah was safe. God had sent a mighty fish to swallow him. Jonah lived in the belly of the fish for three days and three nights. During this time, Jonah prayed to God. He thanked God for letting him live. God heard Jonah's prayers and gave the large creature a command. The fish swam close to shore, opened its great mouth, and tossed Jonah out onto dry land.

Jonah heard the voice of God a second time. "Get up and go to Nineveh. Give the people my message." This time Jonah did as God commanded.

Jonah traveled a long time until he reached the busy city of Nineveh. "In forty days God will destroy Nineveh," Jonah cried. He repeated these words again and again.

The people of Nineveh believed God. They were afraid for their city. Many stopped eating and wore rough rags to show God they were sorry.

God's words reached the king of Nineveh. He rose from his throne, took off his royal robes, and put on rough rags. Then the king sat in ashes. The king ruled that every person and animal should go without food and water. They were to stop behaving in their evil ways. They were to pray to God to forgive them so Nineveh could be saved.

God heard their prayers. The people stopped their evil ways. God forgave them and saved their city. The people rejoiced. Only Jonah was unhappy. Why had God made him travel all this way only to change his mind? "This is what I was afraid would happen," cried Jonah. "You are a good and forgiving God."

"Is it right for you to be angry?" asked God. Jonah did not answer. He left the city. After walking for a while, he sat down and looked toward the city's east wall. He waited to see what would happen next.

God caused a vine to grow over Jonah. The plant shaded Jonah from the burning sun. Jonah was very happy about the vine and the shade it gave him.

Early the next morning, God sent a worm to attack the vine. The strong branches drooped. Its leaves fell to the ground. Jonah awoke to find his beloved plant withered. He was confused over what happened to the plant. Then he noticed an ugly worm crawling on a branch. Jonah knew that God sent the worm. He became angry.

Once again, the sun beat down on the earth. Only this day there was no vine to give shade for Jonah's head. He was so faint he asked God to let him die.

But God said to Jonah, "Is it right for you to be angry about the vine?" "Yes," replied Jonah. "I am angry enough to die."

"You loved this vine that you did not grow. It was only on earth one day," said God softly. "Yet, you want me to destroy Nineveh. I cared for this great city and its people and animals over many years."

Jonah listened carefully. He now understood that God loves and forgives all people who turn to him. It doesn't matter who they are or where they are from.

The Birth of Jesus

In the town of Nazareth lived a young woman named Mary. She was engaged to marry a carpenter named Joseph. He was a good man and was a descendant of King David. Mary would often stop in the doorway of Joseph's shop to say hello. Mary and Joseph loved each other very much, and they looked forward to sharing a long and happy life together.

Long before Mary and Joseph had even been born, one of God's prophets made a very important promise to the world. The prophet said, "An unmarried woman will have a baby boy, and he will be called Immanuel which means 'God is with us.' "

One day, Mary was busy at home when God sent the angel Gabriel to see her. "You are a blessed woman," Gabriel said. "God loves you very much." Even though Gabriel was bringing Mary good news, she was so afraid she couldn't speak. Then Gabriel told her, "Do not worry, Mary. God is pleased with you. You will have a son and you must name him Jesus. He will be called the Son of God. He will have a kingdom that will never end."

Mary asked the angel Gabriel, "How can this happen? I'm not married."

Gabriel answered, "God's Holy Spirit will make it happen. Nothing is impossible for God."

Mary thought a moment and then said, "I want to please God. If this is what God wants, then let it be."

Joseph soon heard that Mary was going to have a baby, and he was upset. He still loved her very much, but he decided that it would be best to call off their marriage.

One night while Joseph was asleep, an angel from God spoke to him in a dream. "Joseph, go ahead and marry Mary. The baby she is going to have is from God's Holy Spirit. After the baby is born, name him Jesus. That means he will save his people from all the wrong things they have done." When Joseph woke up, he went to see Mary to tell her about the wonderful dream he had had. They were married soon after that.

About this same time, the emperor of the country ordered everyone to go to their family's hometown to be listed for tax records. Joseph's family was from a town called Bethlehem, so he and Mary needed to go there to be counted.

They started off on the long journey to Bethlehem. Mary rode on a donkey, and Joseph walked along at her side. The trip was very hard, especially for Mary, because it was time for the baby to come. Finally, they arrived in Bethlehem. Many other people had also come there to be listed for the tax records. The town was very crowded with visitors.

Joseph tried to find a place that he and Mary could stay in for the night, but the inn had no room for them. Finally, Joseph took Mary to a stable because the baby was coming. There she gave birth to a child. She and Joseph named their newborn son Jesus, just as the angels had told them.

Mary wrapped her baby in wide strips of cloth she had brought from home. She gently laid Jesus in an empty manger, a place where the animals ate. Joseph and Mary were very happy.

That same night some shepherds were guarding their sheep out on the hillsides near Bethlehem. All at once they saw an angel from God in the sky. Great light flashed down around them and they were very afraid.

But the angel said to them, "Do not be afraid. I am bringing you wonderful news. This very night a Savior was born for you and your people. He is Christ the Lord. Go and see him. You will find him in a stable lying in a manger."

Suddenly the sky was full of angels who joined together to sing praises to God. "Glory to God in heaven and peace on earth to everyone who pleases God."

After the angels left, the shepherds were very excited. "Let us go to Bethlehem and see this wonderful child," they said to one another.

They went straight into town and found the new baby with Mary and Joseph. The shepherds told everyone they met what the angel had said out in the fields. Mary knew she would remember the shepherds' words about her child for a long time.

The shepherds went back to their sheep, singing thanks to God for the new baby as they went. Everything they had heard and seen was just as the angel had told them.

A little later some wise men who studied the stars came from the east. When they arrived in the city of Jerusalem, they began to ask questions. "Where is the baby who is born to be your king? We have followed his star from the east and we want to worship him."

When King Herod heard about their questions, he was worried. He wanted to be the only king in the land. He called together a group of important men and asked them, "Where will the Son of God be born?"

"In Bethlehem," they answered.

Then Herod called in the wise men and tried to trick them. "After you find the baby, come back and tell me so I can see him too," he said.

The wise men set off for Bethlehem, following the bright star all the way. The star stopped right over the place where Joseph, Mary, and the baby were staying. The wise men went in and knelt down to worship the new baby.

They opened their bags and took out gifts for him. They brought gold, frankincense—which smells like perfume—and myrrh, which is a spice that can be used as medicine. Mary and Joseph were surprised at these rich gifts for the child.

Later the wise men were warned in a dream not to return to King Herod and tell him about baby Jesus. So when they started toward home, they went a different way.

After the wise men had gone, an angel from God spoke to Joseph in a dream. "Get up! Take Mary and the child to Egypt now. Hurry, because King Herod is looking for the baby and will kill him." Joseph, Mary, and Jesus left that very night for Egypt. They stayed there until the wicked king had died.

Then, Joseph took his family back to the town of Nazareth where Jesus grew from a baby to a young man. He became wise and strong and pleased God in all he did.

Stories Jesus Told:

The Prodigal Son
and
The Good Samaritan

When Jesus taught people, he often told special stories called parables. A parable is a story that teaches a lesson. Jesus used these stories to explain the secrets of God's kingdom.

One day, the teachers and leaders of a town Jesus was visiting complained about Jesus. They thought he was spending too much time with bad people.

Jesus answered them by telling a parable about a man with two sons.

Many years ago, there was a man who had two young sons. His sons lived with him and helped on the family farm. Everything was going well, but the younger son grew tired of the work he was doing and did not want to help his father anymore. One day, he said to his father, "Father, give me my part of the property. I am leaving home to make my own life."

The father was very sad because he did not want his son to go. But he gave the younger son the share that was coming to him. The son was very happy when he received the money. He packed up everything he had and made plans to leave home.

Before very long, the younger son went to a country far away from his father's house. He spent his time going to parties and having a good time. He bought himself and his friends everything they wanted. The younger son enjoyed the life he was living and did not think about his father or his older brother.

But the day came when all the money his father had given him was gone. When he had spent everything, he looked for his friends to ask for help, but they were nowhere to be found. About this same time, a famine spread through the whole land. Soon he had nothing to eat.

The younger son decided to look for a job. He went to talk to a farmer. "Do you have any work I can do?" he asked. "I will do whatever you need."

The farmer sent him out in the fields to care for the pigs. The younger son was glad to have the job. He was so hungry that he would gladly have eaten what the pigs ate!

While looking after the pigs, he remembered all the good things in his father's house. Finally, he came to his senses. "In my father's house even the servants eat well. And here I am dying of hunger!"

The son decided to return to his father and say to him, "I have made a big mistake! Please forgive me and let me come back as one of your servants."

As he approached the house, his father saw him in the distance. He ran out to his son and hugged him and kissed him.

The son said, "Father, I have sinned against God and you. I am not good enough to be called your son."

But his father called the servants and ordered that they give his son the best clothes, a beautiful ring, and new shoes. The father also ordered a great celebration to welcome his younger son.

The older son had been out working hard in the fields. When he learned that his father was having a feast to welcome his younger son, he became very angry.

The older son said, "Father, I have always worked for you and you never give me a feast! But when that son of yours comes back after spending all your money, you have a banquet!"

The father answered, "Son, you are always with me and all I have is yours. Your brother made a big mistake but he has returned. I thought he was dead—and he is alive. We must celebrate his return."

Jesus told this parable to help us love and accept anyone who is sorry for the bad things he or she has done.

One day, a lawyer tried to trick Jesus. "The law says that I should love my neighbor as myself, but who is my neighbor?" Jesus answered him with the following parable.

A man was on the road going from Jerusalem to Jericho. He had his goods loaded on a pair of donkeys. As he walked along the road, a group of thieves attacked him. They wounded the poor man and took everything he had. Then they left him half dead lying in the road.

Later, a priest was going down that same road. When he saw the wounded man on the ground, he passed on the other side of the road and did not help him. A little later, one of the helpers in the temple also saw the man who was wounded and lying in the road. He did not help him either.

Then another man from a place called Samaria came along the road. He was a Samaritan, and many people did not like the Samaritans. But when he saw the wounded man, he felt very sorry for him. He washed the man's wounds and bandaged them. The wounded man did not have the strength to walk. So the Samaritan put him on his own donkey and took him to Jericho.

When they arrived, the Samaritan brought the man to an inn. He rented a room and looked after the man all night.

The next day, the Samaritan had to leave. He went out to look for the owner of the inn. When he found him, he gave the owner some money and said, "Take care of the man I brought here. He is badly wounded. If you spend more money looking after him, I will pay you back when I return."

This is how Jesus' parable ended. When he finished telling the story, Jesus asked the lawyer, "Which of the three men acted like a neighbor of the wounded man: the priest, the temple helper, or the Samaritan?"

The lawyer answered, "The one who had compassion and helped him acted like a neighbor."

"That is correct," Jesus said. "Now go and do the same. Love your neighbor as yourself."

This story teaches us to love everyone, even if they are different from us.

Stories Jesus Told:

The Sower and the Seed

and

The Ten Bridesmaids

"Jesus the storyteller is coming!" Children ran to get their parents when Jesus and his twelve disciples came to the fishing village in Galilee. Rumors about Jesus were everywhere. Was it true that he healed sick people? Was it true that he could stop a storm? Were his stories about God really that wonderful? People hurried out into the streets to find out.

Jesus looked at the people gathering and knew that only some of them were ready to trust God completely. Some would follow him eagerly. Others would listen at first and then fall away later. Still others were so far from God they could not even be touched by his words. Sometimes the people seemed like lost sheep that needed a shepherd to lead them home.

As Jesus watched and waited, the crowd around him grew.

Soon the crowd became so great that it was pressing against Jesus and his followers. Jesus climbed into a fishing boat near the shore so that everyone could see him. The crowd filled a whole field. In the distance, Jesus could see a farmer working, scattering seeds on his field. Jesus looked at the crowd and smiled.

He told everyone to sit down, and then he began to speak. "Listen! A man once went out to his fields to sow seeds. He walked all over the field, tossing the seeds in all parts of it. Some of the seeds fell on hard paths made by people crossing the field. Soon birds came and ate them up. Other seeds fell on rocky ground, where the dirt was not very deep. There, the plants grew up quickly but they died in the heat of the sun because they did not have deep roots."

Jesus went on, "The sower kept tossing seeds across his field. Some fell among thorn bushes and weeds. The plants tried their best to grow, but the weeds grew along with them and choked them. But other seeds fell on good soil that was dark and rich and ready. The plants grew strong and made many baskets of grain. If you have ears, listen to what this means!" After he finished telling the story, Jesus' disciples wanted to know what the parable meant.

"The farmer sowing seeds is like me sowing God's Word among the people," Jesus answered. "The hard path is like people who hear God's word, but the devil comes and takes it away, just like the birds that eat the seeds. The rocky ground is like people who have no depth. They are happy when they hear God's Word and it grows for a little while in their hearts. But when following God is hard, they fall away."

Jesus' followers wanted him to explain the rest of the story. He continued, "The bushes and weeds are people who hear God's word and let it grow for a while. But in their hearts they love the world more than God. They love money, clothes, toys, and things to buy most of all. Soon their love for things chokes God's word in their hearts. The good soil is the best of all. It is like the people whose hearts truly love God. They accept God's word and their lives bear more fruit than you can count!"

Jesus' followers were silent. They wondered what kind of soil their lives were like. They looked back where the crowd had been sitting. Not long ago there were hundreds of people gathered there. Now small groups of people stood in circles talking together. Some were coming to Jesus wanting to learn more. Other people walked away shaking their heads.

ow a smaller group gathered around Jesus. He was still thinking about seeds and farming.

"The kingdom of God really is like scattering seeds on the ground," he said. "You plant them and then wait. One day you look and there it is! Grown and ripe! How the seed becomes a strong healthy plant is a mystery!" Everyone knew that people were the same way. For some, news about God was powerful and their lives grew and changed.

Jesus kept speaking. "The kingdom of God is also like a tiny mustard seed. It is so small. Yet when it is planted it grows like magic into one of the largest bushes in the field. Birds build their nests in its branches!"

One day as they walked, Jesus and his disciples heard wedding music echoing over the hills. It was coming from a village nearby. When Jesus arrived, the wedding guests greeted him and invited him to stay. The young bride was standing with some of her friends near the synagogue waiting for her new husband to arrive. Everything was prepared. But the wedding could not start without the groom.

Jesus sat down and began to tell a story. "Let me tell you about the kingdom of God. Once there were ten young women who were going to be in a wedding." Right away everyone became interested. The bride and her girlfriends listened especially carefully.

Jesus continued, "Now five of these women were very wise. But five of them were foolish. Here is what happened."

Jesus continued the story. "Everyone was waiting for the groom. The five wise women brought extra oil for their lamps, just in case the groom showed up late at night. The women waited and waited, and became very bored." Everyone listening nodded their heads.

"When night came some of them sat down and fell asleep," Jesus told the wedding guests. "Suddenly around midnight there was a shout! The groom was coming! All the wedding guests jumped up to meet him and lit their lamps. But the five foolish women saw that they did not have enough oil for their lamps. They begged the wise women, 'Please give us some oil. Our lamps are almost out.' But the wise women said, 'No. If we share with you, we will not have enough for the wedding party. Go buy some in the village.' The five foolish women left the wedding to hunt for oil for their lamps."

Everyone listening to Jesus was very quiet. They wondered what would happen to those foolish women. No one could find oil in the middle of the night.

Jesus said, "While they were gone shopping for oil, the groom came into the wedding hall along with all of his friends. The women who were ready followed them too. The wedding music began to play and everyone danced and laughed. There was plenty of delicious food and wine. When all the friends were inside, the door of the hall was shut.

"A long time later, the foolish women came from the village, tired and sad. They had found no oil and they didn't know what to do. The women could hear the music, so they knocked on the closed door. But the door did not open. They peeked into the windows.

"The women cried, 'Open up the door for us!' They looked at their cold lamps and wept. From inside a servant's voice said, 'I do not know who you are. I cannot open up the wedding for just anyone!' And the door remained shut."

The people listening to Jesus' parable were puzzled. What did it mean? How was this like the kingdom of God?

Jesus explained, "This story tells us that we must keep awake and be ready at all times. We cannot be like the foolish women. Tonight the groom will arrive for the wedding and surprise us. In the same way God's son will return to the world and surprise everyone. Some will be ready. Some will not. And when he comes, only those whose hearts are ready to receive him will be invited to join his kingdom."

Jesus told many stories like the parable of the sower and the parable of the ten young women. In each story he tried to find a way to make people think about how much God cares about them. But he also wanted them to think about their own lives. How much did they love God? Did they have a place for him in their hearts? Were their lives like good soil? Were they ready for the groom to come?

MARTHA, MARY, AND LAZARUS

Jesus traveled throughout the land of Israel for many years. He was very busy teaching people about God's kingdom. He also performed many miracles and healed people who were sick.

Because he traveled so much, Jesus was almost never near his home in Nazareth. Usually, he counted on his friends in other parts of the country to give him a place to stay.

When Jesus traveled in the mountains near Jerusalem, he liked to stay in the village of Bethany nearby. Jesus would hike up the long trail from the hot desert of Jericho. Up he climbed until he could see the rooftops of Bethany above the hills. There he had good friends who were always ready to offer him a bed and meals. Mary, Martha, and Lazarus were their names. They were two sisters and a brother.

One time Jesus came to Bethany after a long trip. Mary and Martha were home, and they welcomed him. Jesus sat in the patio of the house, telling them about God. Mary sat at Jesus' feet listening to every word. But Martha rushed around the kitchen making the foods she knew Jesus liked.

After a while, Martha became frustrated. She came outside and complained, "Lord, it isn't fair! My sister is sitting here while I do all the work! Would you please send her in to help?"

Jesus said kindly, "Martha, Martha. You worry about all the wrong things. Only one thing is really important and Mary knows what it is. This will never be taken away from your sister." Martha was silent. Jesus had made her see that learning about God was more important than worrying about everyday things.

Jesus left Bethany and continued to travel throughout the land. He often went where people did not expect him. Jesus was looking for places where men and women's hearts were ready to receive news about the kingdom of God.

One day when Jesus was traveling through the wilderness with his followers, a young man ran up with a message from Mary and Martha. "Lazarus, whom you love, is very sick," the messenger panted. The sisters wanted Jesus to come right away.

Jesus turned to his followers and said, "Don't worry. This illness will not kill Lazarus. All of this is happening so that God will be praised. And when he is praised, I will be honored too." Some of Jesus' followers still wanted him to hurry to Bethany. But he stayed two days longer where he was.

Finally Jesus decided to return to Bethany. Thomas and a few others warned Jesus, "Lord, we know you want to help Lazarus, but many people in that area do not like you. They might try to kill you there."

Jesus answered, "Lazarus our friend is ill! I must go to Bethany to awaken him!" One follower wondered whether it was a good idea to wake Lazarus. If he was sleeping, didn't that mean he was getting well?

Then Jesus said firmly, "Lazarus has died." Everyone was silent. If Jesus knew that Lazarus was going to die, why did he wait these two extra days? Jesus added, "I'm glad we did not go right away. Now I am still going to see Lazarus and when I do, you will believe in me as you never did before!"

Jesus went to Bethany. Children playing in the fields saw him coming and ran into the village. "Jesus is coming! Jesus is coming!" they shouted.

When Jesus came near, he could hear many people inside Mary and Martha's home crying loudly. Lazarus had been dead now for four days. Martha ran out to meet Jesus in the road. She sobbed, "Lord, if you had been here, our brother would still be alive."

Jesus said, "Don't worry. God will give us life after we die. I am the Lord of Life! Anyone who believes in me—even if they die, they will live again! Do you believe this, Martha?"

Martha nodded. "I believe that you are God's Son, Jesus. You have come into the world from God."

Jesus then told her, "Go inside and get your sister."

When Martha told Mary that Jesus was outside, Mary hurried out onto the road where he stood. She fell at his feet, weeping. "If you had only been here, Lord, my brother would still be alive." Mary hugged Jesus' ankles and cried and cried.

Jesus' heart was moved by Mary's tears. He had loved Lazarus like a brother, too.

"Mary," he said gently, "where have you laid Lazarus's body? I want to go and see his tomb."

Mary led Jesus outside the village to a place where many tombs were cut into the side of a hill. As they walked, Mary noticed that Jesus was crying. She had not realized that Jesus loved Lazarus so much.

By the time Jesus and Mary arrived at the tomb, a group of people had gathered there. Martha was among them. In a loud voice, Jesus called out, "Roll back the stone! Open up the tomb!"

Martha said, "But Lord, Lazarus has been dead for four days. We can't do this."

Jesus replied, "Didn't I promise you that if you believe you would see the power of God? Roll away the stone!"

Several men pushed the stone back. Jesus stood near the opening and prayed, "Father, thank you for always hearing me. Now, please help these people believe when you show your power."

Then Jesus shouted, "Lazarus, come out!"

Suddenly, there was a shuffling noise from inside the tomb. It sounded like a person sliding his feet. Slowly, a man wrapped in burial sheets came out of the cave. He squinted in the bright sunlight.

"Help Lazarus take off these sheets," Jesus ordered the men. "Lazarus is alive!"

The story of what Jesus did for Lazarus spread everywhere. People could not stop talking about a miracle like this. Some of the leaders of Jerusalem even became jealous and wanted Jesus put in jail. They could not see that God was at work in Jesus.

But Mary, Martha, and Lazarus never stopped loving him. Lazarus especially liked to talk about his part. Never again was he afraid of dying. "I've been there," he said, "and Jesus is even more powerful than death."

Not long after he performed this miracle, Jesus returned to Bethany. Jesus knew it would be his last visit. He knew that he would die soon. Mary and Martha prepared a splendid meal for him and invited his very best friends.

When Jesus arrived, he seemed to be in a serious mood. But when his close friends greeted him he cheered up at once.

After dinner Mary brought out a bottle of expensive perfume. It was the kind they had used to prepare the body of Lazarus after he died. Mary poured all of the perfume on Jesus' feet and then wiped them with her long, beautiful hair. The room was filled with the sweet scent of perfume. When they smelled it, everyone remembered Lazarus's death. They wondered if Mary was also preparing Jesus to die.

When Jesus left after his last visit, Martha, Mary, and Lazarus cried as they said goodbye. It made them sad to think that this was the last time they would see him in this life. But they also believed in their hearts that Jesus was the Lord of Life and that even death could not hold him for long.

While he was alive on Earth, Mary, Martha, and Lazarus always made Jesus welcome in their home. They listened to him and loved him with all their hearts. These are the kind of people Jesus calls his friends.

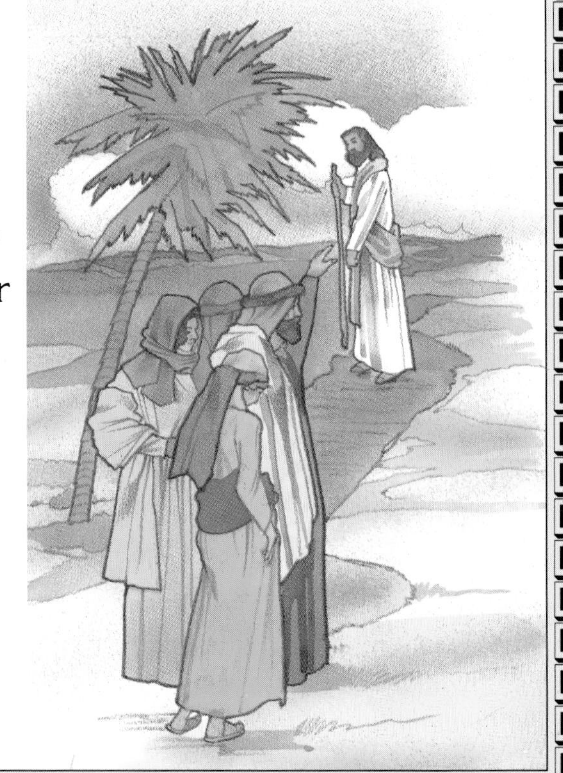

The Miracles of Jesus

After Jesus was baptized, he began to go around the countryside preaching and teaching. He also performed miracles for many people who had special needs.

Jesus performed miracles for rich and poor, for men and women, for Roman soldiers, for those who were sick, and also for his disciples. People began to follow him because they wanted to hear the things he taught and to see the miracles he performed.

But Jesus did not perform the miracles to be seen and admired. He often told the people not to tell what he had done. Sometimes he tried to perform a miracle away from the crowds.

Jesus performed his first miracle at a wedding in a city called Cana. His mother Mary was there as a friend of the family. Jesus and his disciples were also invited.

In the middle of the feast, Mary came to Jesus. “They have run out of wine. Please help them.”

Jesus answered, “It’s all right, Mother. You don’t have to tell me.” Standing nearby were six big stone jars. Jesus said to the servants, “Fill each one to the top with water. Then bring some to the man in charge of the feast.”

When the man tasted it, the water had turned into wine! Jesus’ disciples and the servants knew where the wine had come from. It was a miracle!

Once Jesus was in the town of Capernaum, and an army officer heard about him. The officer had a servant who was very sick, and he believed Jesus could make him well. So the officer asked Jesus to come to his house.

When Jesus was near the house, the officer came out to meet him with a message: "Lord, I am not worthy to have you enter my house. I know you can cure my servant from here if you will."

Jesus was very surprised. He turned to the crowd that was following him. "I have not found this much faith in the whole country! The man's servant is healed."

When the officer returned home, he found that his servant had been healed just as Jesus had said.

Many people wanted to see Jesus and hear him speak. Great crowds began to follow him wherever he went. One day, there was a woman in the crowd who had been sick for twelve years. She had gone to many doctors and spent all the money she had trying to get well again. But instead of getting better, she only got worse.

The woman had heard about Jesus, so she came up behind him in the crowd. She said to herself, "If I can only touch his clothes, I will be well."

She reached out and touched Jesus. At that very moment she was cured of her illness! Jesus stopped and turned around. "Who touched my clothes?" he said.

The disciples with him were surprised at his question. "Look at all these people around you. Anyone could have touched you."

Then the woman came forward and kneeled down in front of Jesus. She was shaking with fear, but she told Jesus the whole story. Jesus said to her, "You are now well because you believe in me. You will not have any more pain. Go in peace."

Jesus and his disciples had gone to the town of Jericho. A large crowd gathered so Jesus and his disciples led them out of town. A blind man named Bartimaeus was sitting and begging by the road. When he heard that Jesus of Nazareth was coming, he shouted, "Jesus, have mercy on me!"

Many people in the crowd told him to hush, but Bartimaeus shouted to Jesus even louder. Jesus stopped and called Bartimaeus to come closer.

"What do you want me to do for you?" Jesus asked.

"Teacher, I want to see again," Bartimaeus said.

"Go on your way," Jesus told him. "Your eyes are healed because of your faith." As soon as Jesus spoke those words, Bartimaeus could see.

Another time, Jesus and his disciples went away to spend some time alone. But the crowds saw them go and followed them. When Jesus realized how many people there were, he welcomed them. He talked to them about the Kingdom of God and cured those who were sick.

As the sun went down, the disciples came to Jesus. "Please tell the crowd to go look for food and a place to spend the night," they said.

"You give them something to eat," Jesus answered.

The disciples were surprised because there were about five thousand people there. The only food they could find was five loaves of bread and two fish that a small boy had brought.

"Tell everyone to sit down in groups of about fifty," Jesus said. When everyone was seated on the ground, Jesus took the five loaves and the two fish. He looked up to heaven and blessed the food. Then he broke the loaves and fish into pieces and told the disciples to pass out the food.

What a supper they had! Everyone ate until they were full. Afterward, the disciples collected twelve baskets of leftovers.

Right after this, Jesus' disciples went down to the Sea of Galilee. They got into a boat and began to row across the lake. Jesus stayed behind to pray.

As the night grew darker, a strong wind began to blow and to stir up the waves on the lake. The disciples rowed and rowed, trying to reach the shore. Suddenly, they saw Jesus walking on the water toward them! They were frightened and thought it was a ghost.

But Jesus called to them, "Do not be afraid. It is I!"

Then Peter said, "If it is really you, I want to walk on the water to you."

"Come ahead," Jesus answered.

Peter got out of the boat and started walking on the water to Jesus. But he became afraid and began to sink into the water.

"Jesus, save me!" he cried. At once, Jesus reached out and grabbed Peter. "Why did you doubt, Peter?"

When they both got back in the boat, the wind had died down. The disciples kneeled down before Jesus and said, "Truly, you are God's Son."

JESUS AND THE CHILDREN

When Jesus began teaching and preaching, he remembered his own childhood. He knew how much his own family had loved and cared for him.

He remembered that they had taken him to Egypt to keep him safe when he was just a baby. After they returned to Nazareth, he helped his father in his carpentry shop. He went to the synagogue to learn how the people worshiped God.

Jesus loved children very much. He always kept a special place in his heart for them.

When Jesus grew up, he would go from town to town teaching people about God. Often, he would help children who were sick or who had other problems.

One day, Jesus was teaching near the Sea of Galilee. A large crowd gathered to hear him. One man in the crowd was in charge of the synagogue. His name was Jairus, and when he saw Jesus he went over and knelt at Jesus' feet.

"My daughter is about to die!" said Jairus. "Please come touch her so she will live." Jesus looked at the man without saying anything. Then he nodded and went with Jairus. Many people followed.

Before they got to Jairus' home, someone came to meet them with sad news. "Your daughter is dead!" they told Jairus. "There is no need for Jesus to come."

But Jesus heard them. He stepped up and said to Jairus, "Do not be afraid. Just have faith!"

They went home with Jairus and saw a crowd of people crying for the dead girl. Jesus went into the house and said to everyone, "Why are you crying so much? The child isn't dead. She's just sleeping." The crowd laughed at his words.

Jesus sent them all outside. Then he took the girl's father and mother and three of his disciples and went straight to where the girl was lying. He held her hand and said, "Little girl, get up!"

And she did! The girl got up and started walking around. Everyone in the room was amazed. The girl's mother hugged her.

"Do not tell anyone what happened here," Jesus said. Then he turned to her mother and said, "Give the child something to eat." There was much happiness in Jairus' house that day!

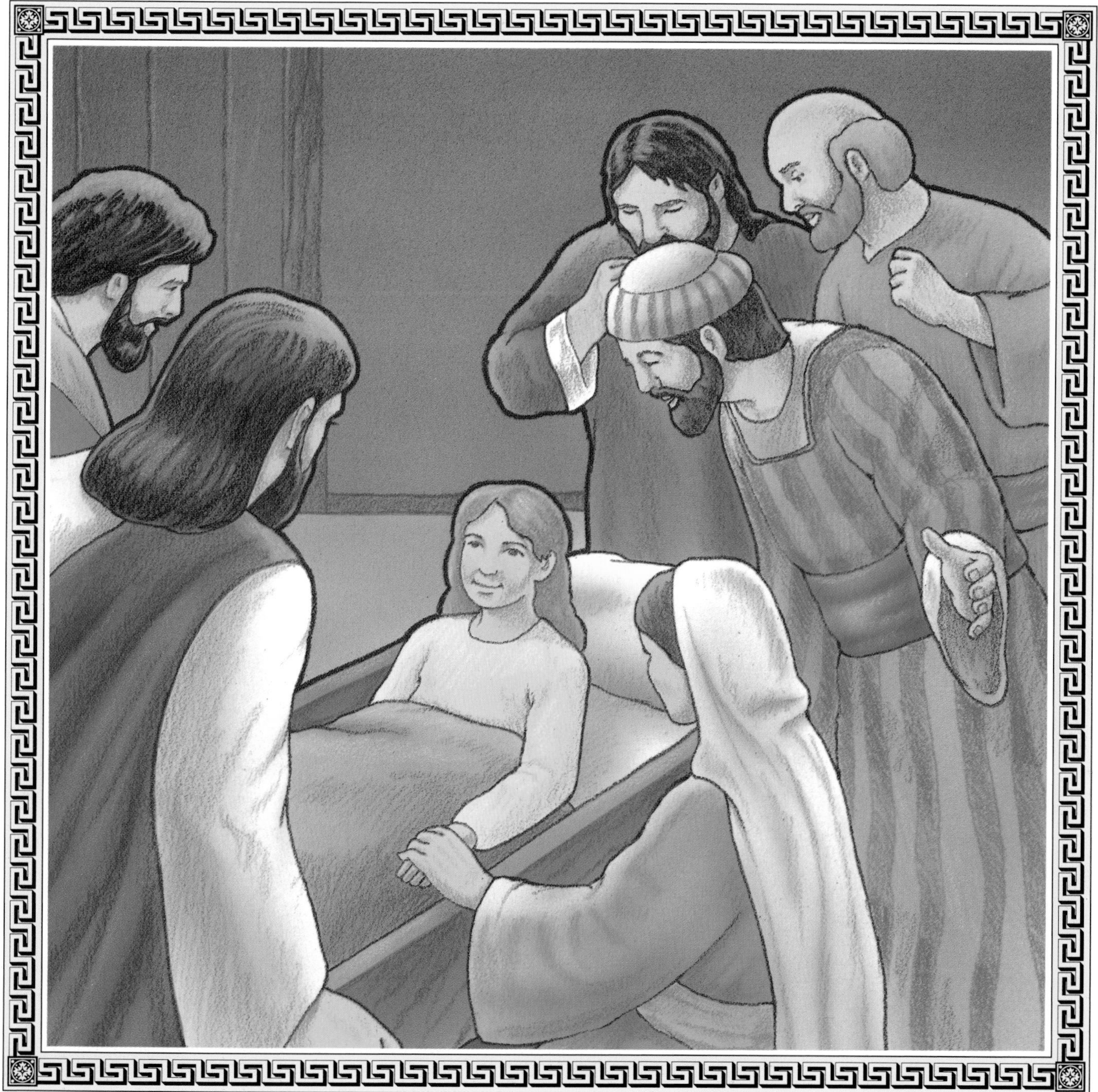

Another day, Jesus was on the road to Jerusalem. He and his disciples were tired. Jesus had been to many places and talked to many people about God's kingdom.

Jesus decided to sit and rest by the side of the road for a while. The disciples were glad to take a break because they had been walking for a long time.

Some people saw the group relaxing by the roadside. They brought their children over to ask Jesus to bless them. But the disciples stopped them. "Jesus is tired. Don't bother him now," they said.

But Jesus saw the children and said to his disciples, "Let the children come to me. Do not try to stop them."

So the disciples stood back and let the children pass by them. The children shyly came closer to Jesus. He smiled and reached out to them. The children came near, and Jesus hugged them close in his arms. Then he blessed them.

"God's kingdom is for children and people who are like them." Jesus said. "Children belong in the Kingdom of God."

Sometimes, children were Jesus' helpers. One day, Jesus and his disciples had gone across the Sea of Galilee to get away from the crowds. But there was a large crowd waiting to hear Jesus on that side as well. Many people had brought their children.

Jesus welcomed them and went up on a high hill to teach them. He told them about God's kingdom and cured those who were sick.

At the end of the day, Jesus' disciples wanted him to send the people away for food. But Andrew, one of the disciples, said, "There is a boy in the crowd with five small loaves of bread and two fish."

Jesus said, "Tell everyone to sit down."

There were about five thousand people in the crowd. After the crowd was seated, Jesus called the boy over and asked him if he would share his bread and fish. The boy smiled and held up his lunch to Jesus. Jesus took the bread in his hands and gave thanks to God for it. Then he began to pass the bread and fish out to the people until everyone had plenty to eat.

The men and women and boys and girls ate all they wanted. Then Jesus asked his disciples to gather up the leftovers so that the food would not be wasted.

One day, Jesus' disciples had an important question for Jesus. They wanted to know: "Who will be greatest in the kingdom of heaven?"

Jesus decided to answer them with an example. A little boy was playing nearby. Jesus called the boy over and asked him to stand in front of the disciples. Jesus put his hand on the boy's shoulder. "Remember this," he said. "Unless you become like a child, you will never enter the kingdom of heaven. Anyone who welcomes a child like this in my name welcomes me."

Jesus went on, "If you want to be great in my Father's kingdom, you must be humble like one of these little ones."

The disciples were surprised, but now they understood how important it is to be simple like a child. They also saw how special children were to Jesus.

The Miracle of Easter

The people who had known Jesus were very sad when he died. The next morning, a man named Joseph from Arimathea went to the Roman governor Pilate. He asked Pilate if he could bury Jesus' body and Pilate agreed.

Joseph took the body, wrapped it in a clean sheet, and prepared it for burial. With the help of others, Joseph laid Jesus' body in a new tomb that had been carved out of solid rock. Then they rolled a large stone across the opening of the tomb.

On Saturday, some of the government leaders remembered what Jesus had said: "After three days I shall rise again." They went to Pilate and got permission to have a special guard watch the tomb.

That Sunday, something amazing happened at the tomb. An earthquake shook the earth, and an angel appeared. He rolled away the stone that closed the tomb and sat on it.

He looked as bright as lightning, and his clothes were white as snow. The guards were very afraid. They trembled and fell down, as though they were dead.

Then Jesus walked out of the tomb. He had returned to life just as he had said he would!

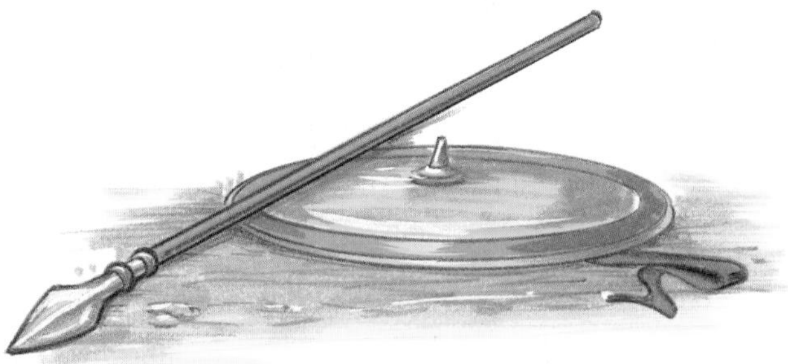

A little later, Mary Magdalene and some other women who had known Jesus came to the tomb. They were very surprised to see the angel in front of the open tomb.

The angel spoke to the women. "Do not be afraid. I know you're looking for Jesus. He is not here. He has risen just as he said he would. Look at the place where his body was laid and see for yourselves. Quickly now, go tell his followers that Jesus is alive again! You will see him in Galilee."

The women were very excited. They left the tomb in a great hurry and ran to tell the disciples.

While the women went to tell the good news, the soldiers who were guarding the tomb went back to the city. They told the religious leaders about the angel who had appeared to them and how the stone was rolled back to open the tomb.

The leaders were very surprised. They talked with one another and made their plan. They collected a lot of money and promised it to the soldiers if they would tell a lie about what happened.

The soldiers took the money and told their captain, "Jesus' disciples came at night and stole his body while we were asleep."

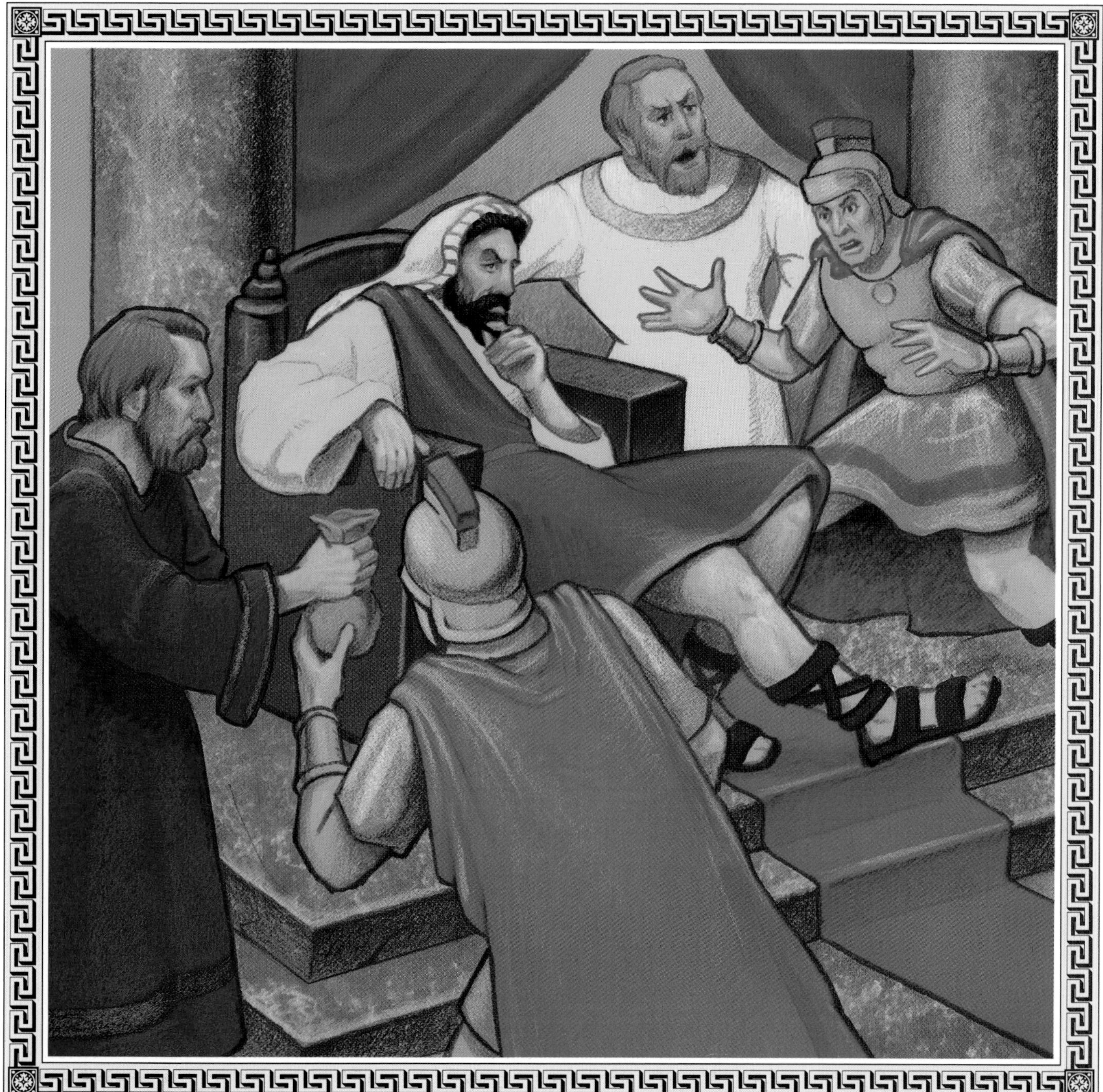

Mary Magdalene and the other women told the disciples the exciting news about the angel and the empty tomb.

Most of the disciples thought the women must be mistaken, but Peter and John ran to the tomb. There they saw the strips of cloth that had been wrapped around Jesus' body, but Jesus was not there. The tomb was empty!

Quickly, they returned to tell the other disciples.

That same day, two of Jesus' disciples were going to a village outside Jerusalem. They were talking about everything that had happened. As they talked, another man came along and walked with them. It was Jesus, but the men did not recognize him.

"What are you talking about?" Jesus asked.

The two disciples stopped and looked at him. One of the disciples said, "You must be the only man in the city who does not know what has happened."

"What do you mean?" Jesus asked.

Then, both of them explained about what had happened to Jesus.

Then, Jesus began to explain everything written about him in the Scriptures, beginning with Moses. The two disciples still did not recognize him. As Jesus talked they came into the village. He acted as if he were going farther, but the two disciples begged him to spend the night with them.

While they were at the table eating together, Jesus took a loaf of bread, blessed it, and gave it to them. At that moment, they knew it was Jesus. Then he disappeared from the room.

The disciples were amazed! They went straight back to Jerusalem to tell the other disciples that they had seen Jesus.

That same night, most of the disciples were together in Jerusalem. The doors were locked. Suddenly, Jesus appeared and stood among them. "Peace be with you," he said. Then he showed them the wounds in his hands and his side.

Thomas, one of the disciples, was not with them that night, and he did not believe the other disciples later when they told him Jesus had been there.

A week later all the disciples were together again, and again the doors were locked. Jesus came to them. He said to Thomas, "Touch the wounds in my hands and my side. Stop doubting and believe!"

Thomas answered, "My Lord, I believe in you."

Jesus smiled at Thomas. "Those who believe without seeing me are really happy."

Jesus told the disciples to go to a hill they knew in Galilee and he would meet them there. They left their place in Jerusalem and went out to the hillside. There they saw Jesus coming. The disciples fell down and worshiped him.

Jesus came closer and began to speak to them. "God has given me power over everything. Now I ask you to go to all people everywhere and make them my disciples. Teach them the things I have taught you. And do not forget, I will be with you forever."

Then, Jesus raised his hands and blessed them. As he was blessing them, he was taken up into heaven. The disciples were amazed.

They went back to Jerusalem and straight to the temple. There they gave thanks to God for the wonderful things that had happened. Then they went out throughout the land to teach people about Jesus anywhere they could.

The Travels of Paul

Before Jesus was taken up to heaven, he told his closest disciples to look for the Holy Spirit. These eleven disciples were called apostles. They picked another man to join them so there would be twelve of them. The twelve and some others who believed in Jesus were meeting together one day. Suddenly, the Holy Spirit appeared to every person in the room. From that day on, the apostles preached and taught about Jesus.

Many people began to believe in the teachings of Jesus—more than three thousand people in just one day! Soon they became known as "the believers," and they began to meet together often to pray and study.

The apostles were meeting and preaching in Jerusalem. The rulers and some other people in that city did not think Jesus was the Son of God. They did not want the people of Jerusalem to become followers of Jesus. So the rulers hunted for the believers and tried to punish them.

One of the people who wanted to catch the believers was Saul. He did not want the believers to preach about Jesus. Saul went from house to house looking for believers. When he found them, he threw them into jail and threatened to kill them.

One day, Saul heard there were believers in the city of Damascus also preaching about Jesus. Right away, he went to the high priest, the head of the religious leaders, and asked for letters to the leaders in Damascus. These letters gave Saul permission to look for believers and to bring them back to Jerusalem as prisoners.

Saul and his helpers left for Damascus. Just as he was about to arrive at the city, something stopped him. Suddenly, a bright light from the sky flashed around him! The light was so bright that Saul covered his eyes.

e heard a great voice from the sky saying, "Saul, Saul, why are you hurting me?"

Saul answered, "Who is speaking to me?"

"I am Jesus!" the voice said. "When you hurt my believers, you hurt me too!"

Saul was surprised that Jesus himself was speaking to him. He was so afraid that he began to tremble. Jesus spoke to Saul again. "Go to Damascus and there you will be told what to do." Then, the great light disappeared.

Saul's helpers were amazed. They had heard the great voice but they had not seen anyone.

Saul stood up and opened his eyes, but he could not see anything. He was blind! His helpers took him by the hand and led him into the city of Damascus. There, Saul thought much about the words of Jesus and the believers he had harmed. He did not eat or drink for three days and spent the time praying to God. While Saul prayed, Jesus sent him a vision, telling him that he would be healed by a believer named Ananias.

After three days, Jesus talked to Ananias in a vision, saying, "Ananias, go to the house of a man named Judas on Straight Street. There you will find a man named Saul from the city of Tarsus. He is waiting for you to make him see again."

Ananias was surprised at Jesus' words. He replied, "I have heard terrible things about Saul. The chief priest has let him come here to arrest any of us who believe in you. I am afraid of him."

Jesus answered, "Go! Do not be afraid of Saul. I have chosen him to be a believer and to preach about me to many people. He will even suffer for me."

Ananias left and went to find Saul as he had been told in the vision. When he arrived, he placed his hands on Saul's eyes and said to him, "Jesus has sent me. He will heal you and fill you with his Spirit!"

Suddenly, something that looked like fish scales fell from Saul's eyes and he could see again! Then, Saul believed that Jesus truly was the Son of God. He was baptized and then Saul was also a believer.

For several days Saul stayed with the believers in Damascus. He began to be called Paul. Right away he began to preach about Jesus. The people who heard him were amazed. They asked, "Is not this the same man who searched for believers so he could put them in jail?"

But Paul kept preaching that Jesus was the Son of God. Some people who did not believe in Jesus became angry with Paul and made plans to kill him when he passed through the gate of the city. They sent guards to watch the gate for Paul.

When Paul heard about this, he asked the other believers for help. After it got dark, the believers lowered Paul over the Damascus city wall in a big basket! And so Paul escaped.

Paul went back to Jerusalem. He wanted to join the believers and apostles there. But the believers were still afraid of him. They did not trust him.

One believer named Barnabas talked with Paul and wanted to help him. Barnabas took Paul with him to meet the apostles. He told them what had happened to Paul on the road to Damascus and how Paul had preached boldly about Jesus in Damascus.

After hearing this, the apostles accepted Paul as a true believer. Paul stayed with them and began to preach in Jerusalem. But once again, those who did not love Jesus tried to kill him.

Finally, the believers sent Paul back to his hometown of Tarsus. He would be safer there.

Later, Paul and Barnabas traveled to many different cities where the people had never heard of Jesus. One day, during this trip, they arrived at an island called Paphos.

When the Governor of Paphos heard that Barnabas and Paul were preaching there, he sent for them so that he could hear about Jesus. But a magician named Bar-Jesus was against this.

Paul was angry. He looked Bar-Jesus in the eye and said, "You are a liar and a cheat. Jesus will make you blind for a while!"

Bar-Jesus fell to the ground, blinded. When the Governor of Paphos saw this, he was amazed. Barnabas and Paul taught him about Jesus and he became a believer.

After this, Paul traveled far and wide teaching about Jesus. In a city called Lystra, he used the power of Jesus to heal a man who had never been able to walk in his life!

Paul's words and his actions helped many people become believers in Jesus.